Burned to
Life

Burned to Life

by

Mel Kenyon

as told to

Bruce A. Darnall
and
Mike Christopulos

DIMENSION BOOKS
BETHANY FELLOWSHIP, INC.
Minneapolis, Minn. 55438

Burned to Life
by Mel Kenyon
with Mike Christopulos and Bruce Darnall

Library of Congress Catalog Card Number
76-1060

ISBN 0-87123-044-5

DIMENSION BOOKS
Published by Bethany Fellowship, Inc.
6820 Auto Club Road,
Minneapolis, Minnesota 55438

Printed in the United States of America

Library of Congress Catalog Card Number 76-1060
6820 Auto Club Road, Minneapolis, Minnesota 55438

CONTENTS

DEDICATION

I would like to dedicate this book to Marieanne for her love and her faith in God through whom all things are possible. Second her faith in me to overcome obstacles and with God's help to get started in the right direction.

Then to my brother Don and to Everett and Frances Kenyon, my parents for their help, support and love.

To the Fellowship of Christian Athletes who strive to make Christ known in the lives of our youth

and

To all race drivers, living and dead, who have contributed to the promotion of auto racing

and

To the glory of God

ACKNOWLEDGEMENT

Special thanks to Bruce Darnell for his enthusiasm and perseverance. To Mike Christopulos for his skill and experience in writing this book.

FOREWORD

Mel Kenyon is one of the best people you would want to meet on or off the race track. He started driving in stock cars, then worked his way through midgets and on to Indy cars. Mel is still one of the best midget drivers in USAC, and has won more midget races than any other driver.

I've always admired Mel's driving ability as well as his courage. In 1965 he was involved in an accident at Langhorne in which he injured his hand. Most drivers would have quit. He had a special glove made so he could continue driving the following racing season. After the fire he did not drive the remainder of the season, but still finished eighth in points.

Mel is one of the great drivers you really enjoy being in a race with because he is always fair on the track.

He is a man everyone likes and admires, and I am proud to have him as a friend.

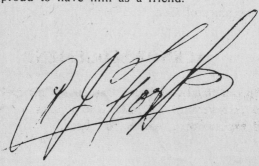

Chapter One

The Fire

Langhorne is a famous race track—for eating up drivers, literally. Little did I dream on that hot, sunny day back on June 20, 1965, that I would be one of the drivers the track would eat up, but that's what happened in the Langhorne 100 USAC championship race.

Langhorne had been a dirt track, but they'd recently paved it. I said to myself, "Oh, what the heck, maybe they have made a race track out of it." So I decided to race there and see what I could do. I didn't have anything to lose. That's what I thought anyway.

Let me say a couple more things about Langhorne. A lot of accidents have been caused there because of the track's centrifugal qualities. Many drivers have been killed there and many others have been injured.

A lot of guys have been leading a race at Langhorne by a big margin but then they've gotten so tired that they've either crashed or had to pull in. It's unlike any other track I've ever raced on.

There's one part of the track they call "puke hollow" because the engines just throw up there, if you know what I mean. The track runs uphill and downhill for a mile around corners. It is very narrow with absolutely no straightaways.

I was driving Dick Kemerly's roadster. It was one of the old dinosaurs that were used just before the rear engine cars became so popular.

On the day before my accident, I did fairly well in practice. I had the ninth fastest time during a practice lap. I wore a new Anson's fire suit during practice. This was a new aluminum-type suit that doesn't breathe. It keeps the air out. But it also gets hotter than blazes in that suit. I was the only driver who wore this suit in May at Indy.

When it came time for Sunday's race at Langhorne, I had to decide whether to wear my new Anson's fire suit or my old cotton suit. The cotton suit was treated with fireproof solutions but this wasn't considered to be much help.

It was awfully hot that Sunday—about 90 degrees in the shade. So I decided to wear my old cotton suit. Looking back, that's about the dumbest move I've ever made. I figured I wouldn't last the race in the new Anson's suit because of the heat.

As things turned out, it got much, much hotter for me, anyway.

During Sunday's qualifying, I placed sixteenth. After the race started, I worked my way up to eighth place when Arnie Knepper lost control of his car and hit the fence. His car burst into flames and pieces of his suspension flew over the fence while they were still burning. This started a fire among some trees near the track and it took about 10 laps to get the track ready for the green flag, and to put out the fire.

I was still in eighth place when the green flag came out. As I came off the No. 2 turn, my motor started rattling badly. I knew it was coming apart. Finally, my engine just blew. A rod had let loose, sawing the engine in two and spilling oil on the tires.

I put on the brakes and raised my left hand to warn the guys behind me that I was in trouble as I headed for the infield. I never got to the infield. I proceeded going out toward the fence. I guess one can blame that on Langhorne's centrifugal force, and the fact that my tires were slick from the oil that had been spilt on them. I spun backward and hit the fence with the left side of my car. When my head hit the roll bar, I was knocked unconscious.

Actually, my car turned about 180 degrees as it bounced off the fence, pointed straight ahead and proceeded down the track. My car had nearly slid to a halt when some real trouble arrived.

Ralph Liquori and Jim Hurtubise had been having their own private battle during the race, and didn't even see the problems I was having as they came charging up lickety-split behind me.

They came bearing down upon me. Liquori hit me first after the wheels on his car and Hurtubise's tangled, breaking Liquori's axle. Liquori's car plowed through my fuel tank, which was mounted in the rear of my roadster, and still contained about 60 to 65 gallons of alcohol and nitro.

There was a rubber bladder in my fuel tank but it broke, spreading fuel all over the track, my car and myself. The fuel burst into flames immediately.

When Liquori's car rammed mine, the impact bent my car so badly it was destroyed even before it caught fire.

The impact jarred my seat belt loose, and I fell down into the cockpit, head first. Nobody could see me. I became the man who wasn't there while my car slid down into the infield where newly-graded dirt almost put out the fire. The cars of Liquori and Hurtubise also came to rest near mine.

Two ex-drivers, who were watching the race, grabbed their five-pound fire extinguisher bottles, jumped over the fence and began spraying their fire bottles on the cars of Liquori and Hurtubise that weren't burning. They couldn't see me in my car. They probably figured I'd gotten out along with Hurtubise and Liquori. Had they sprayed their bottles on my car, it just might have put out the fire because it was nearly out at the time.

It wasn't until Joe Leonard came along and noticed my predicament that those two guys even knew there was someone in my car.

Leonard, who was having car trouble, was driving slower than usual, and saw me slouched in the burning cockpit. He pulled over and ran over to me. He was still wearing his helmet, goggles and fire suit. It's a good thing he was too because the fire in my car had picked up in intensity. Joe managed to unhook my seat belt, but he couldn't pull me out of the car because the steering gear had fallen across my lap. He waved to the two guys to help him.

The three of them pulled me partly out of the car before the flames drove them away. Fortunately, Joe dropped my right arm outside the car when he pulled me up. That act saved my right arm. I'll always be grateful to him for that.

Apparently, I sat in that car about three minutes with nothing on but that cotton suit, before the fire engine arrived and put out the fire. That suit didn't help much. I suffered 40 percent third-degree burns over most of my body. If I had been wearing the Anson's suit I wore at Indy, I wouldn't have been burned at all, except for my hands, All I can say is one lives and learns.

It's a shame they didn't have better ways of fighting fires at Longhorne then. The fire equipment they did have was poor and insufficiently spaced around the track. Also, the ambulance had to travel almost a mile from its station to the accident scene. I'm glad to report, things are much safer at Langhorne now and the safety men wear fire-proof uniforms! However, the champ cars have discontinued running at Langhorne because the drivers did not like driving there.

They did continue the Langhorne 100 that day because the wreck was in the infield. Jim McElreath won.

I was told later that I was talking incessantly in the ambulance, and also in the emergency room at the hospital, rattling on about being burned.

I kept repeating, "Lord, I'm burned. Lord, I'm burned." But I don't remember any of it. The last things I remember were my motor vibrating badly, and putting my left hand in the air to warn the other drivers.

The next thing I remembered was waking up in the hospital about 3 o'clock the next morning. When I came to, Herb Miller, a professor at the University of Michigan and a very good friend of mine, was dropping bits of ice into my mouth. Boy did that feel good!

Until my accident at Langhorne, I'd been very lucky. The most serious injuries I had suffered in racing were a cut on my chin at Vallejo, Calif., in the spring of 1965, and a sore neck from a flip in 1964 at San Jose.

The hit   The fire

They don't see me

Chapter Two

The Recovery

Right after Herb dropped those bits of ice in my mouth, I realized I was wrapped up like a mummy. All I could see was the end of a finger, and the thumb on my right hand.

I had been taken to Lower Buck's County Hospital near Philadelphia. Herb and his daughter had been at the race at Langhorne, but had left early because they just didn't like that track. They were leaving when they heard over their car radio that I'd been involved in an accident. Another good friend, Bob Higman called my wife, Marieanne, and my brother, Don, who then called my parents and friends.

Marieanne and Don had returned to our home in Davenport from Fort Wayne the previous Friday, after I had run in a midget race at Fort Wayne. Both of them flew from Moline to Philadelphia. Herb picked them up at the airport. I didn't see Marieanne or Don until Monday morning.

Months later, I was told that the hospital was jammed on the night after the crash. There was a rush of race fans and drivers wanting to see how I was. It was a mob scene. The hospital wasn't big enough to handle such a big crowd, so they asked them all to leave.

When I woke up Tuesday morning, the blisters were sticking out from the cracks in my bandages. I didn't feel much pain because they kept me doped constantly. Two special nurses took care of me around the clock. I only stayed in that hospital near Philadelphia about a week, but it cost me nearly $1,500.

Marieanne stayed with me, but Don had to leave after a few days. He went back home and tried to figure out what to do about the midget car I'd been driving. Don got Mike McGreevy to drive our midget for the rest of the year.

My injuries were quite extensive and most of them stemmed from the fire, rather than the impact of the crash itself. I'd been burned on most of my left leg, the bottom part of my right leg, my left arm and hand, and on the left side of my chest.

Near the end of the first week, the only way I could get my bandages off was to soak them. To do it, I had to sit in a tub of water. The bathroom was so small that nobody could help me get into the tub.

I had to do it myself. The pain was simply awful while I was climbing into that tub. After I soaked myself, a doctor cut off the bandages, and also the blisters and loose skin to drain the liquid and relieve the pressure. After he'd finish, I'd climb back into a wheelchair and go to my room to be rebandaged.

While I was in that hospital, many different people from all walks of life, some of whom I didn't even know, tried to get permission to have me moved to the San Antonio Veterans Burn Center.

People from USAC and Firestone, along with Johnny Rutherford and John Mecom, Jr., president of the New Orleans Saints football team, worked hard in my behalf.

I wasn't a veteran, but I received special permission from General Curtis Lemay, who was then chief of staff, to enter the San Antonio Burn Center.

The Firestone people sent their twin engine Lockheed plane to fly me to San Antonio. Some seats on the plane were removed and I was placed on a pad on the floor of the plane. Marieanne, and one of the special nurses from that hospital near Philadelphia, Mrs. Jacqueline Trofe, flew with me to San Antonio.

The nurse gave me one shot on the plane to ease my pain. When we landed at the San Antonio Municipal Airport, an ambulance was waiting for me. They drove me directly to the Burn Center. They didn't waste any time.

They took me straight to the burn center's physical therapy department and submerged me in 90 degree water in a Hubbard stainless steel tank, which was shaped like an enlarged human.

They did this in order to soften the scabs, blisters and bandages so they could be cut away from the burned flesh more easily. The doctors used a straightedged-razor to shave off all the scabs, blisters and bandages. They started at my feet and worked up.

I didn't say a word or complain once while they were doing this. The doctors told me they were very proud of me for not yelling while they were shaving me. I wasn't as brave as those doctors thought. I couldn't feel a thing. "Little did you guys know, but I had a pain shot just

17

before I got off the plane," I admitted to the doctors a bit sheepishly.

The first week I was at San Antonio, they kept me in an intensive care, isolation ward. They wanted to make sure I didn't bring any new diseases or infections into the place.

I was allowed three pain killing shots during my first week at San Antonio. After that, only aspirin. I guess they don't want their patients to become addicted to those pain-killing shots.

I was delirious my first week at San Antonio. They had this routine where they'd put you in a circular bed and make you lie on your back for three hours. It wasn't my idea of fun. Far from it.

One night while I was lying on my stomach, I called out to a nurse:

"You can unhook me now, I'm ready to go home. Fun's fun and all is well."

I'd been talking in my sleep. When I saw a nurse hovering over me, I woke up with a start. Only then did I realize where I was. Naturally, the nurse didn't let me go home!

After the first week, I was moved into a ward. There were no walls in the ward. There were four beds to each cubicle, or 28 beds in all.

The hardest part about being a burn patient is the debriding process. That's where they strip the burned skin away from the good flesh. After soaking in a tank of water for an hour or so, a doctor then pulls and snips the burned skin away from the good skin with a tweezer or scissors. This was so painful. I remember one time it hurt something awful. I hollered myself hoarse and loosened several teeth after biting down so hard on a rolled up wad of gauze I'd stuck inside my mouth.

I'll never forget the first time I went outside while I was in the hospital. I was as excited as a small kid on Christmas morning. Marieanne took me on a wheelchair ride to a pleasant garden area behind the hospital. I was in this old, rickety, wooden wheelchair, which was covered with sheets. They used the sheets so the sun wouldn't blister me.

Marieanne was wearing hard soled shoes, which didn't hold well as she was pushing me down a ramp onto the garden area. There was about a two-foot decline on the ramp. Marieanne slipped and almost lost control of the wheelchair. I got a lump in my throat as my wheelchair skittered crazily along, and nearly flew off the ramp.

I could see the headlines now, MEL KENYON, RACE DRIVER, BADLY HURT IN WHEELCHAIR CRASH. Fortunately, we made it down to the bottom in one piece.

I'm glad to say my next ride outside was a much more pleasant one. It took place in a Volkswagon, which Marieanne drove. Bill Smyth, former executive director of USAC, owned a Volkswagon dealership in San Antonio then. He and John Mecome saw to it that Marieanne had the use of a Volkswagon while she was staying in San Antonio.

Marieanne was living at the guest barracks about a mile from the hospital. Having that Volkswagon sure made it easier for her to get around. And it made me feel a lot better, too. She took me for several rides around San Antonio. I must admit, however, that it was pretty difficult for me to get in and out of that Volkswagon.

I was getting along very well at the time. I called home to tell them I'd be able to come home in about two weeks. They had some bad news for me. They told me that Hal Schroeder, a good friend of mine, who helped me get started in racing, had just committed suicide. His funeral was to be in three or four days.

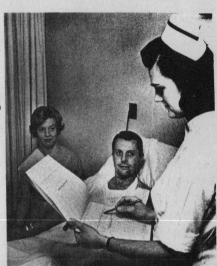

16th operation

"outside" San Antone Burn center

The joy of a Volkswagon ride

Chapter Three

My Buddy: Hal Schroeder

Hal had been suffering with a kidney ailment for some time. When they told me he had killed himself, I was stunned. I stopped feeling sorry for myself and started thinking about all the good times Hal and I had together.

We were bosom buddies, although Hal was about 15 years older. I first met him at a roller skating rink in Bettendorf, Ia. Hal was managing the rink, and I used to go there to skate about five times a week. I became very good friends, not only with Hal, but with his wife and the crowd he hung out with.

Hal and his brother-in-law owned a stock car. I bought out his brother-in-law's interest in the stock car. We called the car the "Old White Ghost" because it was so old and white, I guess.

About a year later, the "Old White Ghost" died—literally. It conked out. Hal and I decided to build a new one. Hal was living out in the country then. There happened to be the hull of a burned-out house next door to Hal's place.

We used the basement off that burned-out house as a storage area. We built our new car out in the yard. Our next project was even a bigger one. We decided to build a new house for Hal, using the shell of the burned-out house as a starting point. We had a great time tearing out the inside of the burned-out house. Hal and I had this little game to see who could knock down the biggest section of the house, using a sledge hammer. Hal usually got the best of me in these contests because he was so strong.

I got out of the hospital a week early so I could attend Hal's funeral. The date was September 10, 1965, nearly three months after my fiery crash at Langhorne. The Bear Manufacturing Company was very nice and flew me in its Twin Beach aircraft from San Antonio to Davenport for Hal's funeral. It felt good to be out of the hospital, but all I could think about while we were flying to Davenport was Hal.

I just wish he hadn't done it. Hal was the type of guy who was very proud. He wouldn't ask anybody for help. Even when he had a hernia, Hal would still go out and lift the biggest log he could find—by himself. That's how he was.

But this kidney thing really knocked him for a loop. He became allergic to the fluids they cleaned the kidney machine with and which they used on him. As a result, he didn't heal properly when they put some tubes in his arm to hook up the machine. He was in constant misery. Hal couldn't go up more than three steps before he would have to stop and rest for a few minutes.

Until he became sick, Hal was so strong and agile that he could do anything in the world. And I mean anything. Even though he had only one eye, he was fantastic. He could do anything he wanted, in any sport or race car. You name it and he could do it—hunt, ride motorcycles, race cars. He couldn't do any of those things after he got sick. I think that's the thing that really got to him.

When they told him they would have to move the tubes from his legs to his arms, he coudn't accept this latest piece of bad news. He decided to end things then and there. I'm not saying what he did was wrong and I'm not saying it was right. Hal couldn't stand the pain any longer and he put himself and everybody else out of their misery.

Maybe if Hal had waited until I got home we could have both been miserable together. Who knows? Maybe, I could have helped him over his problems because I had a different outlook on life than he did. I'd talked to Hal on the telephone several times when I was in the hospital. But it seems I was talking to everybody on the phone in those days. I do know our telephone bill was running about $120 to $140 a month.

I found out later that after they told Hal that they would have to move the tubes from his legs to his arms, he made up his mind to leave the hospital. He went back to his room and got dressed. Even though the pain must have been killing him, he somehow walked down to the parking lot, got in his car and drove the 65 miles from the hospital to his home in Davenport.

How he ever did that without passing out, I'll never know. When he got home, he stuck a 12-gauge shotgun on his chest and pulled the trigger. The 12-gauge did a good job. He was dead within the hour.

We were bucking a terrific headwind in the Twin Beach craft while we flew to Davenport. We knew we were going to be late, so the people in the beach craft radioed ahead to the Moline Airport, asking them to furnish a police escort for us. In turn, the airport people called the funeral home and asked them to delay the start of Hal's funeral for 30 minutes. When we landed at Moline, the Illinois police whisked us away to the Mississippi River where the Iowa police took over and escorted us to the funeral home. We arrived at the mortuary just a few minutes after the services started. I had trouble sorting out my thoughts during the funeral. I kept thinking about what a great person Hal was.

After the funeral, we went home and were met by a room full of reporters. Reporters were the last people in the world I wanted to see. I was extremely tired from my long day and besides, Hal's death and funeral were still too fresh in my mind to think much about myself.

But you know how reporters are. They're pretty stubborn and won't stop bothering you until you agree to answer their questions. They all wanted to know if I hoped to race again. I told them, "If the good Lord is willing, I will race again." I had no doubts in my mind that I would get back into racing. Of course, reporters had asked me the same thing when I was in the Burn Center at San Antonio and I had told them the same thing, then too.

When I was in San Antonio, everyone was very nice to Marieanne and I. We received 1,175 cards and letters from friends and fans. Many of the people I got cards and letters from I didn't even know. I did really appreciate their thoughtfulness, however. And I also was very thankful for the financial contributions I received. I couldn't have gotten through that difficult period without the support of all these people.

Various cards, a real help

My special glove

Chapter Four

On the Comeback Trail

All the doctors at the Burn Center advised me to forget about racing and go into some other line of work. Racing was in my blood, however, and besides I didn't know anything else I could do better than drive a race car. I certainly didn't want to become a factory worker again. I hated factory life. I spent five years working in a factory and I don't know how I lasted that long. I nearly ruined my eyes doing it.

I must say I'm fortunate to have a wife like Marieanne. I became her first baby. She did things for me when I was in the hospital that you'd normally do for some small child. Her love for me never diminished even after the accident left me with a grotesque stump on my left arm. Her love for me was and has been a constant source of inspiration. She stuck by me through my trying ordeal, never once complaining. When you find somebody like Marieanne, you've found a super person. I desperately wanted to return to racing after I got out of the hospital.

Even though we'd been married only a year, she had no qualms about me getting back into racing, if that's what I really wanted to do. She was willing to back me. We've been married over 10 years now, and it doesn't feel like more than a couple of weeks.

We both had faith that if I was physically able to race again, God would give me the strength and guidance to do so. When I did return to racing, I had a different purpose other than just fame and fortune. I still wanted to win races, but I also wanted to use myself as a witness for my Lord.

A week after I returned to Davenport, Marieanne, Don and I went to Anderson, In., for the last midget race of the 1965 season in the midwest. Mike McGreevy, who drove our midget most of the time after my wreck, did very well.

The next day, we went to the Hoosier 100, a 100-mile championship dirt car race in Indianapolis. I'd never seen the race before. I walked down pit row, wearing a big sombrero, and with my collar turned up. I had a white handkerchief wrapped around my fingerless and vulnerable left hand to keep it shielded from the sun. Everybody was glad to see me. Joe Quinn, the promoter, gave us good seats in the grandstand for the race, which was won by A. J. Foyt.

After that, Don and I went west for the windup of the midget season. Tommy Copp drove our midget and finished second at Vallejo, Ca. Tommy was third in the Grand Prix at Gardena, Ca. We had a good year with our midget. I'll have to give Don a lot of credit for that. He worked like a beaver to maintain it and haul it to the races, He'd never worked on engines alone before. He kept in constant touch with me by telephone while I was in the hospital at San Antonio.

Mike won the midget driving championship that year. Even though I drove in only 19 of the 53 races before I was burned, I finished eighth in the point standings. Our car won 11 feature races and set 17 records. I set 14 of those records and Mike the other three.

We returned home the last week in November, and I entered a hospital in Davenport for an operation on my left arm. Some tissue had formed on my left shoulder and elbow, limiting the mobility in my arm. Dr. John Syverud, a plastic surgeon, took some skin from my thigh and grafted it to cover the openings left by the removal of the tissue.

When I got out of the hospital, I was so weak that about all I could do was walk. Before my accident, I weighed 155 pounds. Afterward, I was down to 135. I was a mere shadow of my self. To build myself up, I began working out in a private gymnasium owned by Stan Sparling in Davenport. I worked out twice a week. When I started, all I could lift was eight pounds, and I was fortunate to do that. Three months later, I was lifting 55 pounds with one hand! I was in the best shape of my life.

In addition, Dr. Clay Thompson, a chiropractor, gave me free treatments until I was financially on my feet again. I'm indebted to Dr. Thompson and Stan Sparling, along with the many, many other people and friends who offered me assistance and encouragement.

During the off-season, Don, my dad and I completely rebuilt our midget in preparation for the 1966 season and my return to racing. Our car was sponsored for the second straight season by Andy Grantelli and STP. We painted the car and it looked very sharp. That left us with one major problem. How was I going to use my disabled left hand on the steering wheel? My dad and Don sat in that car for long periods, trying to hit on a solution. I never really gave it that much thought. What we finally came up with was a glove and socket affair. It proved to be so efficient that we haven't changed it since I started using it in 1966.

We welded two pins together to form a "T" pin and clamped it on the steering wheel with two hose clamps. My dad then made me a socket, which was attached to a leather glove. This glove in turn fits over the "T" pin and is locked in place.

I'm still running with the original glove. It was made in an upholstery shop in Moline. The second glove was made at a shoe store in Davenport. I use the second glove for big car races and the first one on the midgets.

Now that I had my trusty glove and socket gadget, I was ready for my return to racing. It took place in March at Tucson. I was ready. I felt like I'd never really been out of racing. Marieanne and my folks wanted to go to Arizona to watch me, but they couldn't make it. Marieanne was still working, trying to pay all of our bills. Don and I went to Tucson. Johnny Rutherford was there and he told me, "Take it easy, you don't have to go so fast, so quick."

But I told him, "I'm comfortable, why not?" I felt at home in the car and had no problems. The glove device worked perfectly. I was second in the trophy dash and second in the heat race. During the feature, the steering gear bracket broke and I had to hold the gear up and steer at the same time. I still managed to finish fifth. That made me very happy.

The next night we went to Phoenix. Before the race, we welded the bracket back on at Bud Trainer's Arizona Hard Chrome Company. The midget race at Phoenix was held the night before the championship car race there. There were a lot of important racing people in Phoenix for the big car event. They'd come early to swap stories, renew acquaintances and get ready for the start of another big car season.

They saw me try my luck on the half-mile track at Phoenix, which is a fast, fast track. I broke A. J. Foyt's track record by over a second, and also established a world's track record for a half-mile dirt track! This was only my second race since the fire. I won my heat race and finished second behind Chuck Rodee in the feature. I was elated. I knew I was on my way again.

I'm comfortable

"Pit stop"

BOB HARKEY 28 BRYANT HTG. & COOLING SPL. ATLANTA FALCON SP

Chapter Five

Another Chance at Indy

One of the people who watched me race at Phoenix was Fred Gerhardt, a well-known championship car owner. I had an opportunity to become acquainted with him. Then in April, I went to Fresno, Ca., and competed in a 100 lap midget race. It was my good luck that Gerhardt was also at Fresno.

Mike McGreevy and I really put on quite a show for Gerhardt. We were bumper to bumper most of the race. We swapped the lead several times until Mike finally won. I came in second, right on his bumper. My strong showing convinced Gerhardt he ought to give me a chance to race at Indianapolis again. I'd passed my rookie test at Indy the previous year in 1965, and came close to making the 33 car field. I averaged 153.5 miles per hour during my qualifying run, and my time held up until I was bumped on the final day of qualifying by Bill Cheesebourg. Naturally, I was anxious to race at Indianapolis again and make up for my disappointment of the previous year.

Gerhardt and I worked out a deal whereby he gave me permission to use his two-year-old rear engine car that George Snider and Gordon Johncock had driven the two previous years. The car hadn't been rebuilt or set up for this year and we didn't even have an up-to-date engine to put into it. All we had was an old 255 Offenhauser engine. For some reason, we called our car, "Old Ironsides." Considering everything, that name was as good as any.

I had a car but I didn't have a garage at Indianapolis to store it in because I was a late entry. Besides that, I didn't have a license to drive big cars. I only had a license to drive midgets. The people at USAC wouldn't give me a "big car" license until I'd proved myself.

We went to Indianapolis on May first, and solved our first problem when we temporarily took over Jim Hurtubise's garage. His car and backup car hadn't arrived yet. It had been two years since I'd last worked on a large Offenhauser engine. It was like starting all over again. We overhauled the engine and put it back together to meet USAC's approval.

Nobody had ever driven at Indy with a handicap like mine. A lot of guys went to bat for me, especially A. J. Foyt, Don Branson and Chuck Rodee. Rodee probably had as much to do as anybody for me getting my license back. He'd raced against me. The others hadn't. The first thing USAC officials wanted to check out was my glove. The medical director at the track inspected my glove and socket affair carefully.

So far so good. The next thing I had to do was take my car out for a shake down spin and see how it felt. I completed the shake down with no problems. Now came the hard part. Since I'd never driven a rear engine car before and hadn't ever qualified at Indy, I had to take a refresher test. I wanted to take my refresher test right after the shake down but USAC officials said, nothing doing. It was too windy. They postponed my refresher test for 24 hours.

The weather was beautiful the next day. I had a strange feeling in the pit of my stomach as I prepared to take my refresher test. I didn't know it at the time, but refresher tests are generally taken in traffic. For me, however, USAC officials waved everybody else off the track. They still had doubts about my ability to drive again. A lot of people had faith in me though. They showed that they really cared by sending me all sorts of medals. I received both Catholic and Jewish medals and good luck charms. And people of various protestant denominations wrote me, offering words of encouragement. My family and I said many prayers before I climbed into my car for the refresher test. We asked the Lord to give me guidance and strength.

Once I got out on the track, I felt confident. My faith was very strong. I just knew I was going to pass. Once I started, however, I had no idea how many RPM's my motor was turning because my tacometer was broken. All I could do was listen to my engine and check the three shut off points used at the end of each straightaway to help me judge my speed. Don kept giving me information in the pit on his blackboard. Don told me I was going a little too fast on my three practice laps. I slowed down to try to stay within the three-mile-per-hour-limit.

On my third practice lap, Don flashed me the word

35

"Test" as I passed the pit area. That told me that on my next lap, I'd be on the first phase of my refresher test. This phase consisted of running 10 consecutive laps within a three-mile per-hour-limit without a miss. I ran 10 perfect laps and Don gave me the signal to go into the second phase of the test. Once again, I ran 10 more perfect laps.

I felt pretty good about things when I met later with drivers who had been stationed around the track to observe and evaluate my performance. They all told me I did quite well and had passed the test. One driver did suggest that while I was warming up, I should keep my wheels as close to the white line as possible. In this way, I'd give other drivers room to run in the main groove without slowing down. I took his advice and even today I make it a point to do this. It upsets me when other drivers don't give me the same courtesy.

Now that I'd passed the refresher test, all I had to do was qualify. We put in a lot of work on Old Ironsides, getting her ready for the qualification runs. Old Ironsides was perking along real good and handling like a dream. On the morning of the first qualifying day, I hit a speed of 160 miles per hour, an unheard of speed for a normally aspirated engine, especially a 255.

I was calm and at ease as I went out to qualify. I knew the Lord was with me. On my first lap, I hit 157 miles per hour. I hit 158 miles per hour on the second lap, 159 miles per hour on the third and 158 miles per hour on the last lap. That gave me a four lap average of 158.5 miles per hour and earned me the seventeenth position in the Indy 500 field. I'd made it! So had Jim Hurtubise, who was also driving for Fred Gerhardt. Jim had been badly burned at a fire at Milwaukee the previous year. So here we were, the "burn twins" about to race in the famed Indianapolis 500. You can imagine how happy I felt, considering what had happened to me at Langhorne.

My folks and Marieanne were in the grandstand near the starting line on the day of the big race. The pace car, driven by a Mr. Firestone, almost smashed into the pit entrance because several cars couldn't get their engines cleaned out when the green flag was dropped.

As a result, there was a messy first lap pile-up on the straightaway to mar the start of the race. Seventeen cars were involved and 11 of them were knocked out of the race! Wouldn't you know it, but I was right smack dab in the middle of it. Don Branson was ahead of me and his car took a wild sashay on the track. I had no choice but to miss Branson, or else plow right into him with a full load of fuel. I jerked the car violently to miss Don and this put it into a reverse spin. My car slammed into the wall backwards. The left rear wheel smashed into the wall, breaking the wheel and flattening the tire. My car bounced off the wall and was left completely broadside as cars came thundering down upon me. If you've ever watched movies of this famous Indy crash, you know the Lord had to be guiding those drivers who were involved in the pile-up. Cars shot past on both sides of my car, scraping the wall and sliding around it. Miraculously nobody cracked into my car. No one was seriously hurt.

The only thing that happened to me was the fact my glove was torn off my hand, along with several layers of skin. Right after my crash, several medics came running up to me and poured some methylate on my hand and put a couple of bandaides on it. Quickly, I stuck my hand back into my glove. I didn't want anybody to look at it and decide I couldn't drive because of some little scratch on my hand. Nothing was really wrong with my car except for the flat tire. Marieanne saw the whole wreck. When it happened, all she could do was cry out, "Oh, no, not already!" They put a new set of tires on my car and I was able to get back into the race while the yellow flag was still on. The car handled kind of funny. I learned later that one of the radius rods buckled about one quarter of an inch. The race proceeded without incident after that first lap crash. My car was running smoothly, the damaged rod notwithstanding. Graham Hill won the race, but he and I were running on the same straightaway most of the afternoon.

With some 70 laps to go, I pitted for the last time. I must have picked up some matter in my refueling tank because as soon as I got back on the track, I dropped a cylinder. It plugged the nozzle completely, thank goodness. If it had only partially plugged it, it would have burned a hole in the piston and I'd have been through for the day. As it was, the cylinder was plugged completely, forcing me to run on only three cylinders. This slowed me down considerably, and caused my pit crew and myself to wonder on which lap I'd be forced to drop out. Crank shafts just don't last when something goes wrong. More often than not, they break and come apart. Mine vibrated very badly, but fortunately it stayed intact the whole distance. Good Old Ironsides!

I completed 495 miles, or 198 laps and finished fifth, some five laps behind the late Graham Hill. This was the highest finish in the Indy 500 for one of Fred Gerhardt's cars. We received $23,000, which was the most I'd ever won in a race. I was tickled pink.

A week after the 500, we went to Milwaukee where I finished seventh. The next big car race was at Atlanta on a high banked track. During the 10 practice laps while I was driving at speeds of over 165 miles per hour, I spun my car completely sideways. I straightened it out in time to save it, but I realized I didn't have the strength to run at this track. We were running at such great speeds that we were bottoming out very hard and wearing out our cars.

It took a lot of strength to drive under those conditions, strength I didn't have. I couldn't get my head back far enough to see anything except the track. I told Mr. Gerhardt I honestly didn't think I had enough strength to drive. He left the choice up to me. Tommy Copp, who had driven our midget in California the previous year, asked if he could fill in for me. He'd worked for Mr. Gerhardt earlier and although he'd never driven a rear engine car before, he wanted to try it. Mr. Gerhardt agreed to let him take my place in the Atlanta race. Tommy did so well after only 15 practice laps, that we put him into the qualifying line. He qualified with a speed of 157 miles per hour. That was a very good speed, considering his inexperience with rear engine cars, and the difficulties of racing on that high-banked track.

Race day was hot. We rigged a water cooler and put it between Tommy's feet, so he could suck on water while he was driving. I warned Tommy to be careful because the car accelerates much faster with a full load of fuel than other cars do. I also pointed out to him that since it was a 300 mile race, he could take his time learning the track and getting the feel of the car. Evidently, he didn't hear a word I was saying. When the green flag fell, Tommy passed six cars on the first straightaway and then lost control of the car in the second turn. He stuffed it into the wall! When the car hit the wall, it sounded like a small atomic bomb going off. A few minutes later I was talking to another burn patient in the emergency room. His face, hands and legs were burned pretty badly. Later, most of his face and nose had to be rebuilt and his hands required grafting. It was like Langhorne all over again. Tommy Copp had joined our growing "burn" club.

The initial blast tore off the outside fuel tank on our car and sent it hurtling over the wall. We didn't have much left of our first rear engine car. It was one big pile of junk. About the only thing we could save was the engine. We packed all the rest of the scrap and sent it on to Mr. Gerhardt in California. I don't imagine he enjoyed receiving it.

Chapter Six

My Early Years

I was born on April 15, 1933 in DeKalb, Il., to Mr. and Mrs. Everett Kenyon. I was their first child, and a depression baby at that. My folks wanted to name me Mel but my grandmother insisted that I be called Melvin. My parents compromised. They officially gave me the name Melvin, but they've always called me Mel. The only time I use Melvin is when I'm signing something official.

Things were tough in those days. My father was an automobile mechanic in DeKalb, but he couldn't find any work there so we moved to Cedar Rapids, Ia., when I was two years old. My dad got a job at Cedar Rapids maintaining and repairing refrigerators, which were very new at the time. Shortly after we moved to Cedar Rapids, my brother, Don was born. Three years later, my sister, Marcia, was born. Our family never had much money when I was growing up, but we had something else that was even better—love and understanding. We were a very close family then and still are. My dad was very conservative. My mom was more liberal. She saw to it that I received a lot of things, which I wouldn't have gotten if it had been left up to dad—things like my first bicycle, my first motorcycle, etc.

Don and I wrestled each other and carried on like brothers do, but we never really fought. I don't think we've had more than a couple of arguments for as long as I can remember. We have different temperaments. Don has a terrible, terrible temper while it takes an awful lot to get me angry. One time when I was around eight years old, Don and I were playing outside near a new house that was being built. We started throwing clods of dirt around. I picked up this big clod and threw it as hard as I could. I wasn't really aiming at Don, but he stuck his head out at the last minute, and the clod smacked him right in the eye. He started screaming and crying and carrying on so much I thougt I'd put out his eye. We ran home and told my folks what I had done. I felt pretty bad and scared at the same time. My dad was waiting for me with a big belt when I got home. He whacked me with that belt real hard several times. This time, it was my turn to cry.

We never had many new clothes but my mom kept the clothes we had clean and well patched. When I was in grade school, the kids used to call me, "Hoppy" because I wore some tall boots. We had a large half-acre garden near out house, and it furnished us with most of our food. We also had rabbits and some banty roosters that gave us eggs. Our neighbors weren't too happy about that, and complained so much that we had to get rid of the rabbits and chickens.

While I was growing up I became very interested in

mechanics. Like father, like son I guess. My dad had all sorts of tools and compressors lying around and he let me help him when he was doing odd jobs. I was more of a hindrance than a help. But by watching dad, I did pick up a few pointers. He told Don and I we could use his tools as long as we would wipe them off and put them back where they belonged. If he ever found the tools we'd used dirty or misplaced, he wouldn't let us use them again for a while. My dad and I used to overhaul toys that we'd gotten. I still have some of those toys and they are in good shape.

My dad sometimes worked 18-20 hours a day to keep the family going. My mother did her part, too, canning all sorts of fruits and vegetables from our garden, and baking delicious pies and cakes. Don and I also did all kinds of chores around the house and elsewhere to earn extra money. We needed the money to pay back our folks for the things they would buy us. Our parents would give us money to buy such things as a bicycle, motorbike, motorcycle but they would always insist we pay them back later. I'm glad they did that. It made us appreciate hard work and taught us the value of money. When they loaned me the money to buy my first bicycle, I got a paper route to earn money to pay them back. When I was 15, I purchased a motorbike. It cost much more than a bicycle. I wasn't earning enough money on my paper route to pay for the motorbike, so I had to get another job. My next job wasn't exactly what I had in mind but it did bring in more money.

For the next two summers, I worked at a cemetery, mowing grass and digging graves! Cutting the grass wasn't too tough, but digging those graves sure was. I'll say one thing about being a grave-digger, it keeps you in good shape. It would take two of us about three hours to dig a grave. And we'd have to go all out to finish the job in that amount of time. Digging a grave is monotonous and backbreaking. The guys I worked with invented this little game to make time go faster. We'd time each one of our grave digging efforts and then try to beat it the next time we dug a grave. If you're wondering if I felt "spooky" or "scared" about working in a grave yard, the answer is No.

When I was going on 17, I figured it was time to graduate from the motorbike class to motorcycles. Don and I borrowed some money from our folks and each of us bought a motorcycle. At the time, we had a single car garage which was unheated. During the winter months, we'd take our motorcycles and store them in the basement. Before we'd take the motorcycles downstairs, we'd empty their gas tanks. That is when the fun began. What we did after that was foolish and reckless, but fun just the same. Our basement stairs were steep. The motorcycles weighed about 150 pounds each. We'd take the motorcycles, one at a time, aim them down those steep stairs, grab hold of the front wheel brakes and let go. Then, either Don or I would race down the stairs, lickety-split, hoping to get to the bottom before the motorcycle crashed into the furnace. Sometimes we'd stop the motorcycle in time and sometimes we wouldn't.

Our motorcycles survived those hard winter knocks and provided us with a lot of use. Often, we rode them from Cedar Rapids to Davenport, a distance of 75 miles.

Riding motorcycles and motorbikes were right up my alley, but driving a car was something else again. When I was quite young, Don and I fashioned a pushcart out of orange crates. Until I was 17, that's about as close as I'd come to driving a car. My first driving experience took place at Camp Wapsy Y, a YMCA camp near Cedar Rapids. I'd worked there a couple of summers, washing dishes and setting tables.

There was this old panel truck that was used at the camp. I never got a chance to drive it but I did a lot of work on it. One day, my mom and dad came out to the camp to visit me in their 1937 Ford. My dad had been trying to teach me to drive, without much success I might add. I asked him if I couldn't drive our Ford around the camp area, pointing out there weren't many other cars around. After a long pause, he agreed to let me drive his Ford. My first solo spin wasn't something to write home about. For the life of me, I couldn't let up on the clutch smoothly. When I did, I stomped on the gas pedal too hard. I had that car bucking and leaping every which way. My dad must have thought he was watching somebody try to ride a bucking bronc. Despite my poor debut, my dad didn't ground me. Every time, he and mom visited me that summer at camp, my dad would let me drive his car. After a while, even I became proficient at shifting gears and making the clutch and gas pedal do what they were supposed to do. I got my driver's license the next summer. And this time, I got to drive the truck to pick up provisions and haul things around Camp Wapsy.

My very first car

Mechanic for camp wapsie "Y"

Chapter Seven

School Days

I wasn't a Rhodes scholar or anything like that in school. I had trouble concentrating and remembering things. I started school in Cedar Rapids. Dad had gotten a job in Davenport but he commuted from Cedar Rapids for three years. Finally, we found a home in Davenport and moved there when I was in the ninth grade. Probably my worst subject in high school was English. I couldn't understand it and still don't. I did well in shop and gym. By the time I graduated in 1951, I was getting some A's and B's. It was a struggle to get through school. Sports weren't a big thing with me, either. Oh, I did run the dashes in track and wrestle in the 135 pound division. But I busted up my knee while I was practicing football during my junior year, and that ended my athletic career. Later, my old knee injury kept me out of the service.

Since I wasn't a big jock or brain in school, I wasn't a

ladies man. I was very shy. I didn't date much in high school. In fact I don't think I kissed a girl until I was a senior. I had my chances, too, but didn't really know how to act around girls. One time this girl, whose father was a florist, gave a coke party at her house. Her parents were gone for the night. I suppose something could have happened that night, but I didn't know how to go about it. A lot of the guys in high school smoked and drank beer. I tried smoking once but didn't like the taste it left in my mouth. I also didn't like the taste of beer. I never smoked or drank after that.

In high school, I was quiet and considered a listener. People, mostly girls, would tell me their problems. I could have started an advice to the lovelorn column, I guess. Although a lot of girls talked to me and poured out their problems, I never got up enough courage to ask any of them for a date. I didn't start to become popular with the girls until after I bought my first car from Dick Elliott. It was a 1937 Ford that had been used in stock car racing. It had a roll bar in it, and the fenders were trimmed just a bit. Because the car had been raced a lot, the doors didn't fit too tight, and the cold air whistled through the car. Fortunately, it had a good heater.

My dad wasn't too keen on the idea of me buying a reclaimed stock car. For one thing, we were always short of money. and he was a bit reluctant to loan me any at this particular time. But because Don and I had always been good about repaying any money our folks had loaned us, dad had set up a special savings account for us. We could borrow from this account and then pay him back with no interest. It took a lot of talking on my part, but dad finally agreed to loan me $325 to buy my first car.

A short while later, my dad's insurance company got wind of the fact that I'd bought a reclaimed stock car. That didn't set well with those people. They cancelled the insurance for our whole family! My dad was really upset. He had a right to be. He'd been with them for 12 years and had a clean record. He'd never made one single claim and now they cancelled us all out just because I owned a reclaimed stock car.

My dad wasn't mad at me, and I was thankful for that. My dad, Don and I were able to get insured with another good company, Travelers. Owning a reclaimed stock car made me a minor celebrity in high school. The girls began flocking around me. I was still bashful and the girls knew it. They also knew how to take advantage of me. Every time they would ask me to cart them some place, I'd jump at the opportunity. I thought they liked me, but they really only liked my car.

That car provided me with many good times. One of the funniest things that happened in it took place at our senior class picnic. Our picnic was held at the Davenport Fairgrounds. There was a quarter mile track on the opposite side of the grandstand near the picnic area at the fairgrounds. I'd watched races there for years. For some strange reason, the gate to the track was open on the day of our picnic. It didn't take me long before I was trying to promote a race. I talked 15 other guys into racing around the quarter mile track. Naturally, I had a big advantage. I had the only car that was cut out for this sort of thing. I grabbed the lead right away as we tore around that dirt track at speeds of around 60 miles an hour.

Dirt and dust were flying all over the place, our

classmates were yelling their heads off, cheering us on, and the principal and assistant principal were on the verge of having heart attacks. Around and around the track we flew, faster and faster, with me in the lead.

Finally, the assistant principal, Mr. Hempstead, could take it no more. He came out onto the track waving this big, dirty handkerchief at us. There was no way we were going to stop, not then. We still had several laps to go. Mr. Hempstead kept edging out onto the track more and more, pleading with us to stop before anybody got killed. He edged out onto the track so far that he was in real danger of being run down. Fortunately, I won the race before that happened. Mr. Hempstead was red-faced and livid as our cars headed out the gate. When we got the cars stopped, he ran up to us and mumbled something which nobody understood. Then he turned and talked to the principal. I still think he was in a state of shock. None of us was punished, and I've never figured out why we weren't.

My first victory in a race, unofficial as it was, did have one bad effect. Just before I stopped my car, I noticed that it was very, very hot and the temperature gauge was sky high. I parked the car under a tree in the picnic area. I started to unscrew the radiator cap when the radiator blew up and the cap smashed up against a tree. My little spin around that dirt track resulted in a cracked block and I had to rebuild the motor.

I was able to drive my car most of that summer. I filled the radiator full of water after it blew up. And everytime I changed oil and put in five quarts, I'd also fill up the radiator with water. At periodic intervals, I'd have to put more water into the radiator. This puzzled me. I checked the oil level and it was always to the top.

What was happening was that every time I'd drain the crankcase, I'd drain out about 10 quarts of water and maybe one quart of oil. I thought I ruined the whole motor. When I broke the motor down, I discovered that the water was acting as a fairly good lubricant. The motor was in good shape, except for the block.

Like I said earlier, I never was a ladies man in high school. Even though I now had a car, I rarely dated. I didn't go to our senior prom. It wasn't because I didn't know how to dance. Our family often went ballroom dancing. I didn't go to the prom because I didn't get around to asking anybody. The night of the senior prom my buddy and I—I forget who it was now—were out cruising around town in my '37 Ford. We were stopped for a red light and I noticed two girls in a '49 Ford alongside of us. One thing led to another and pretty soon we were drag racing them all over the Quad Cities. I hate to admit it, but I lost. We decided to park one of our cars and ride together. It would have been pretty tough to get four people into my coupe, so we went in the girls' car.

It turned out that the girl driving the car was named Carol. She was from Moline, and was driving her brother's car. Carol and I hit it off real well that first night, we started dating on a pretty regular basis. Later, we became engaged. We didn't break up until five years later. We broke up about the time that I'd really been bitten by the race driving bug. I didn't have enough time to spend with Carol and she resented it. She started going with somebody else. That was the end of my first big romance.

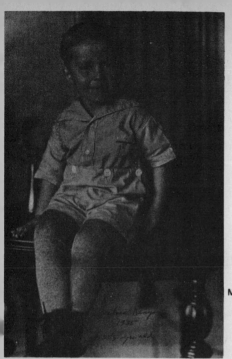

Mel at 2½

Brother Don, sister Marcia and Mel

Mel and camp truck

Chapter Eight

A Race Driver Is Born

When you're young, everybody asks you, "What are you going to be when you grow up?" With me, I never said I wanted to be a fireman, policeman, pilot or anything like that. When I was 13 years old, I made up my mind that I wanted to be a race driver. The idea of being a race driver first hit me one morning when my brother Don and I were walking to Sunday school. We passed this gas station, and at the station we saw this sleek midget race car. The crew had stopped to gas up. They still used gas on midgets in those days. We didn't know it then, but there was a race track about five miles from our house in Cedar Rapids, and the midget was going to race there.

My eyes just about popped out as I gazed longingly at that car. It was fantastic. It was an old homemade car, painted silver with a big red "O" painted on it. After Sunday school, we couldn't run home fast enough to ask our dad if he'd take us to the races that afternoon. He said he would. That was my introduction to racing. The races were held in Marion, a small town near Cedar Rapids, at a small dirt track called Seymare Acres. Two things happened that day that I still remember. During qualifications, one car flipped completely over, and the driver put his arms out while his car was upside down. It looked like he was trying to help his car get back on its wheels. I thought it was a pretty neat trick. Now I know better. It's a scary and dangerous thing to do when a car flips.

I found out how scary and dangerous racing could be during the last lap of the feature race. A driver, Harley Phillips, was killed in the race. The wreck actually occurred after the checkered flag. Harley Phillips took the checkered flag and then turned around to see who was behind him. That was a big mistake, I learned later. His car spun sideways and he was rammed from behind by another midget. Phillips then rolled sideways and flipped end over end. The car landed on top of him, pinning him to the steering wheel. He died instantly. I heard after that this was to be Harley Phillips' last race. He was a very sick man and had only six months to live. He was planning to retire from racing. In a way, you might say his death was a fitting end. I guess it was better than dying in bed. He didn't even know what hit him.

We talked about Harley Phillips' death on the way home. The next day I cut pictures of the crash from the newspaper. I still have those clippings. His death, however, didn't dissuade me from my ambition to be a race driver. That was the first time I saw somebody die in a race. Much, much later when I was racing myself at Marion in 1963 I had a driver, Shorty Templeman, practically die in my arms. I was running second in this particular race. There was a big pile-up behind me and cars and debris were strewn all over the track. As I came around the track, I noticed no one was even close to Shorty Templeman's disabled car, trying to help him. They were working their way up through the tangled wrecks. I stopped, got out and went over to get Shorty out of his smashed up car. He was in a bad, bad way. It took a couple of guys and I quite a while to pry Shorty out of his car. He died even before they could put him in the ambulance. Naturally, his death shook me up. That night I had a time sleeping. I realized, though, this sometimes happens in racing. Dying or getting killed in a crash is not necessarily all that bad. It's harder on the people you leave behind.

After I graduated from high school, I decided to get a steady job. My first steady job was working at a Shell Station in Davenport, which was owned by Dick Schanden. I was the manager of the station. Sort of. Out of the clear blue sky, Dick Schanden fired me. That really made me mad. I asked Dick why and he couldn't give me a straight answer. He hemmed and hawed and said all sorts of things that didn't jibe. I learned later that the reason he fired me was because he wanted to hire a good friend of his to take my place. Getting fired was one of the best things that ever happened to me. I worked for two more gas stations before I got a real good job with Bendix Aviation as an apprentice burnishing operator. I operated a delicate Swiss machine. Most of the pieces I worked on were small enough to go into wrist watches. I was a pretty good man at my job. My old high school shop experience came in handy. I could read blueprints and micrometers very well. I was so good that I was promoted from apprentice to a full operator after I was on the job only a month!

The people I worked with didn't like this. They didn't like it either that I did my work so fast. The bosses at Bendix had hired some "experts"—time and study people, they were called—to figure out ways of doing our work more efficiently. Now these guys didn't know a hill of beans about these new Swiss machines. They were at the mercy of the operators. All of the other operators drug their heels and did less work than they could have done. Consequently, the time and study people set low quotas for our machines. But me, being the eager beaver that I was, produced as much work in as short a time as possible. I got to the point where I could turn out my day's quota in two or three hours! That posed a dilemma for the bosses. Either they had to set up new quotas to conform with my rate of production or else find a new position for me. They wisely, I think, chose the latter course and promoted me. They made me a setup man. Now a setup man prepares 22 machines to be used by other workers. It usually takes one to three years to become a setup man.

I stayed at Bendix Aviation for five years. I'd work hard during the week and on weekends I'd often go to watch races with Dick Elliott. Elliott was racing several cars. I kept asking him if I could drive one of his cars. But he wouldn't let me. I couldn't blame him. After all, who wants to let an inexperienced driver drive a $5,000 race car.

While I was working at Bendix, I met Hal Schroeder at the roller rink and bought out his brother-in-law's interest in a stock car. I desperately wanted to become a race driver and figured that the only way I could do it was to buy my own car. My folks weren't very happy about it. I think they'd have been much happier if I'd taken up the violin or ukulele. Hal and I were partners now in a stock car operation. He drove the car and I maintained it during the first two years of our partnership in 1952 and 1953.

Finally, I got a chance to drive my first race. It took place at Freeport, Il. We'd been running our car there all season in 1954. In fact, Hal had the championship wrapped up going into the last race of the year. Hal was driving our car that day and I was driving one owned by Ray McMurray. McMurray's car was a 1937, six-cylinder Chevy coupe. I'd never driven anything that big or heavy before, but I was doing quite well. I'd moved up into the top 10 when I blew a tire during the feature race. I didn't know I'd blown my left rear tire as I came down the home straightaway heading for the pits. My car was acting funny, fish-tailing all over the place. I lost control as I approached the main grandstand. They had this fence made out of old railroad ties protecting the grandstand. My car climbed that fence, rolled along it for a while, flipped over, and then came down the other side—on its wheels, if you can believe that. The car was a mess, and so was I. I wasn't wearing gloves because I didn't expect to drive that day. What a mistake that was. My hands were all raw and sore from gripping down on the bare steering wheel so hard. I had blisters on top of blisters. I counted 11 separate blisters. My racing helmet, of which I was so proud, was all nicked up and bent out of shape. Sad to say, Ray McMurray had to junk his car. I'd received a royal initiation into racing. The day wasn't a complete loss. Hal won the feature and our car took the championship for the season.

My first stock car

Winning modified in Rockford IL

"OLE 98"

Chapter Nine

My Second Season

Hal and I continued our partnership in 1955. He was still our driver, though, and a good one, a natural. One of the best. Even though I'd wrecked Ray McMurray's car the previous year in my ill-fated debut, he was impressed with my driving skill. He asked me to drive his car. I jumped at the chance.

I was a busy guy that season, maintaining and doing all the work on our own car and driving Ray's. It was a good arrangement, except for one thing. As good a driver as Hal was, he simply couldn't tow our stock car to the races. We towed the car on a four-wheeled tandem trailer. Hal tried to tow it once but he had the stock car whipping and wandering all over those very narrow, bad roads of those days. He wound up in the ditch. I figured it was time for me to come to the rescue. I volunteered to tow our car and leave the actual driving to Hal. That meant that once we got to a track, I had my work cut out for me. First, I'd get our car ready for Hal to drive. Then, I'd drive Ray McMurray's car, and after each race, it was back to my towing duties again. I never let Hal forget this, either, constantly reminding him, "Oh well, we can't all be perfect."

During this period, I was still a setup man at Bendix. They asked me to be a shop foreman. I turned them down. Too much politics was involved. My bosses at Bendix knew that I was a race driver, and they were nice enough to give me time off to race as long as I gave them enough notice. It finally got to the point, though, where they told me I would have to choose between my job and racing. I wanted to continue doing both. About a week before I was scheduled to get my two weeks vacation for that year, I quit Bendix and went to work for Dick Elliott.

I didn't do badly in 1955 driving for Ray McMurray. I picked up a few bucks and more important than that, I gained some needed experience and learned a whole lot about racing. Meantime, Hal Schroeder continued to do his superb job of driving—on the track—for us, and he brought home some money to keep our partnership going.

A couple of "firsts" happened to me in 1956. I got married and my parents saw me drive in a race for the first time. In the spring of that year, I met Betty. She worked at Bendix. We were married later that year and bought a house trailer, which we moved out to Hal Schroeder's place. The marriage didn't last. Betty didn't like racing. She was very nervous and couldn't stand to watch me drive. Out of the 100 or so races I drove during the time we were married, I don't think she saw more than five. That meant we were separated a lot. We grew further apart and finally separated and got a divorce in 1957. It's something one isn't proud of, but it was probably the best thing for both of us.

I did okay in my first race of the season in 1956, finishing third in a feature. I talked my parents into coming to watch me race my next time out at Freeport. Naturally, I was excited about this and wanted to impress my folks, especially my dad. He had never been too keen about me becoming a race driver. I visualized myself winning the race, earning the plaudits of the crowd, and going up to my dad afterward to get his congratulations.

Things didn't exactly work out that way! My first race before my folks had all the overtones of a Mack Sennett comedy. Hal was leading this particular heat race and I was right on his bumper. We received the white flag and headed down the back straightaway. Just as we came into the No. 3 turn, a driver "Num" Lauring got a bit anxious and fouled up all my ambitious plans. He veered down into the grass and then came back onto the track, hitting me broadside. My car flipped three times sideways and five times end over end before it came to rest on top of a high fence. I knew I had to get out of that car in a hurry before it caught fire. As dazed as I was, I managed to struggle out of the car. It was a long way down from that high fence to the ground. As I stepped out of the car, I tore out the seat of my pants. You might say I was more embarrassed than hurt. When the ambulance drove up to get me, I had trouble seeing. Seems that when I took off my leather helmet, a piece of the leather part got stuck on my eyes, partially blinding me. I didn't know this at the time, though.

As the ambulance was leaving the track, it swung in

front of the grandstand. I had the presence of mind to stick my head out of the ambulance and wave to my folks. I wanted them to know I was okay. People in the stands must have thought Who's this dingy character with a black leather strap over his eyes waving at everybody? On the way to the hospital, we came to a four-way stop. The driver turned back to us and said, "Hang on to the cot, we just lost our brakes." We whizzed through that intersection without hitting anybody. How we ever made it to the hospital in one piece I'll never know, but we did. At the hospital, they checked me over and there was nothing really wrong with me. I just needed a couple of stitches in my elbow and ear. After they stitched me up, I hitched a ride and got back to the track in time to see the feature race. I made sure, though, that I first tore off that leather strap over my eyes. Hal won the feature in our car. As for the car I was driving, it was a piece of junk. About the only parts that weren't damaged were the roll cages and the place where I'd been sitting. The trunk and front and rear axles had fallen off, and the engine and radiator were smashed to smithereens. On the way home from the track, Hal drove while I lay down and rested in the back seat. I was pretty sore for a couple days.

Near the end of that summer, Hal sold his interest in our stock car to me. He had a chance to drive for someone else. He wouldn't have to put up any of his own money or work on the car. He felt he couldn't afford to pass up this opportunity. At about the same time, the people who owned the tandem trailer we used to haul our stock car around, told me they needed it and I couldn't use it anymore. There I was with my own stock car, but without a trailer to haul it, and without a partner. Betty's brother came to my rescue. He was a farmer and let me use his hayrack to haul my stock car. You heard right, I said hayrack. It was on a John Deere four-wheel-gear. I worked on that hayrack to make sure it wouldn't wander all over the road like hayracks often do. I put lights on the hayrack. I'll admit it looked pretty silly to see a stock car on a hayrack being towed down the highway. But that's how I hauled my stock car to the tracks the rest of the 1956 season, and the following year.

I really kept my first stock car in tip-top shape. If it received the slightest scratch or was bent in any way, I straightened the car out and painted it. It was never a rust bucket like so many stock cars are these days. I had over $3,000 invested in that car, and I was very proud of it.

After I bought Hal out, I began driving the car myself. It handled much better than most of the other cars I'd driven. Like Hal did in it before me, I won my share of races. In fact, I won so often that a lot of the tracks didn't care to invite me back. Hal ran into the same problem when he was driving the car. Other drivers had bigger cars with bigger engines. But I don't think any other car handled like mine which had a flat-head Ford engine. Usually, I was the only driver with this type of engine. Most stock cars then were Chrysler V-8's, Cadillacs and Chevrolets. They simply couldn't beat me on dirt. On high-banked asphalt tracks, like Rockford, they had the horsepower advantage and did beat me. I won the dirt championship in 1957, and finished fifth in points on asphalt tracks.

My first home built midget

"51" Blue Devil

Chapter Ten

My First Midget

My brother Don was discharged from the Air Force early in 1958. He came home with all that mustering pay, just waiting to be spent. It didn't take me long to figure out a way for him to spend it. I talked him into being my partner on a midget car. We bought a midget car from Dick Elliott, which I'd helped Dick build. I really didn't have to do much talking. Don became very mechanically inclined while he was in the Air Force. He started out as a crew chief and later on became a flight engineer. He knew a lot about cars.

That was the start of a beautiful partnership, which continues to this day. By then, I'd sold my stock car but drove it occasionally for the fellow who bought it. We took our midget to Rockford for my first midget race. We got to Rockford a day early. It's a good thing we did because the engine wasn't running smoothly. The magneto and condenser were giving us problems. Don and I figured out a way to set the timing of the magneto and correct the condenser. The next day, I didn't have a very good qualifying time but did run in the heat race and semi-feature.

When it came to driving a midget, I realized I didn't have much experience. Because of that, I decided to start last in the heat race instead of in my qualifying position. When the race began, I was content to lay back and see what developed. Coming off the first turn on the second lap, I charged right up the middle of the track and took the lead on the straightaway. I led from then on until the last lap. I probably would have won except for the fact I sheared an axle and had to drop out with a little over a lap remaining. We had a spare axle and were able to put it on in time for me to run in the semi-feature. Dick Elliott, who was watching the race, helped us put on the new axle.

When the semi-feature started, once again I chose to start last because of my inexperience. Soon, however, I was challenging for the lead. I came within a whisker of passing the leader at the checkered flag. Only my inexperience prevented me from winning. After the race, Dick Elliott, who'd never let me drive a car for him, told me I might make a good midget driver after all. That made me feel pretty good.

We took our car home and Don painted it a beautiful shade of blue. We went to Rockford again the following week. I was feeling pretty cocky, remembering how close I'd come to winning my first midget race the previous week. I took third in the heat race and qualified to run in the feature. There were 18 cars in the feature. I started in the No. 12 spot. During the race, there was a three-car pile-up ahead of me. I slowed down as I approached the wreck, but like a fool, I looked back to see what had happened. That was a big, big mistake. One of the cars involved bounced off the fence and I slammed into it. The impact stood my car right up on its nose. Everything in my car was bent out of shape except for the tail and rear bumper. To top it all off, the engine slid forward and disengaged itself from the drive line. There was the engine, in that bent chassis, idling away like nothing happened. Our new car was just three weeks old and it was a pile of junk. Fortunately, I wasn't hurt but that race brought my head down out of the clouds and convinced me I still had a lot to learn about driving a midget.

We rebuilt that car but it wasn't handling too well at first. Finally, Don and I got the midget running smoothly and decided to race it at Sun Prairie, Wi. Elver Lund, a good friend of mine whom I'd met at Rockford, talked me into going to Sun Prairie. I'd never run the midget on a dirt track before like they had at Sun Prairie. I'd been to Sun Prairie many times but only as a mechanic for Dick Elliott. I won my first race at Sun Prairie and finished second in the semi-feature. Don and I made $58 over and above expenses. We thought that was super. Fifty-eight dollars was a lot of dough in those days. Why, it was almost a week's pay. As happy as Don and I were over my successful debut at Sun Prairie, our night was saddened by a tragedy. Elver Lund broke his neck and died instantly when his car climbed the wall and landed upside down on top of him. Elver was the first friend I'd seen die in a crash. I accepted Elver's death as part of racing. It didn't dampen my enthusiasm for the sport.

Our rebuilt car started giving Don and I problems about this time, so we decided to sell it and buy a Curtiscraft midget in the winter of 1958. I raced it all over the midwest in 1959, and even managed to beat Billy Woods in a trophy dash at Sun Prairie, Wi. Woods was then the No. 1 driver and champion in the Badger Auto Racing Association. He was a real charger and beating him did a lot for my ego.

That first winter we bought the midget, I competed all over Florida. I did poorly, as might be expected. The tracks in Florida were much different than the tracks I'd been used to. It was harder to get traction on them. I did much better when I returned to Florida in 1959 and continued to do well there the next two years.

In 1961, we bought another midget. That year was notable for a couple of reasons. Don had his one and only fling as a driver, and we had a slew of accidents. You name it and I think we had it happen to us in 1961. I upended my car once and extensively damaged it. Our new car was demolished not once but twice by two other drivers. And we had 11 engine explosions during the year! When we bought the second car, I began an active campaign to persuade Don to become a driver. Before he went into the service, Don wouldn't go across the street to see a race. Finally, I convinced Don to try his luck at driving in a race at Cedar Rapids. He did very well in his very first race. He had the sixth best qualifying time, which earned him a spot in the trophy dash.

Dick Ritchie, one of our good friends, had blown an engine during qualifying and was without a car. He was a top-notch driver and asked us if he could drive our second car. We told him, Okay. We were short of cash and figured he could earn some for us. Besides, Don decided that racing wasn't for him. "Those darn cars go too fast for me," he told me. Now, I'm sorry he didn't run in the trophy dash because we'll never know how he'd have done. Dick Ritchie won his heat and took second in the feature. He brought in the only money we won that night. I broke a crankshaft in the feature and had to drop out.

From that day on, Don decided to stick to mechanics and leave the driving to me. You might say, he's the real backbone of our 3-K Racing. He has the business head, keeps the books and is our chief mechanic. He builds the chassis and maintains them while I set up the motors.

You know how they say that two brothers should never go into business together because they'll constantly be fighting. Well, that's not true in our case. Don's not only my brother and partner, but he's my friend. He's not the least bit jealous of my attention or praise I might get as the driver in our team. We got along well when we were growing up and it's carried over into racing. We have no problems whatsoever. He's got his views on certain things and I've got mine. If we can't agree, we'll compromise. My dad has been part of our 3-K operation since he retired. Ever since 1967, we've maintained our shop and lived in three trailers in Lebanon, a small town outside of Indianapolis.

Indianapolis is the center of racing and being located close by makes it very handy for us. Don spent a lot of time finding the place we're living at now. We own about 3 1/2 acres of land. On it we grow all sorts of vegetables and Don's wife, Lynn, and Marieanne and my mother can them. Don, my dad and I probably spend about 12 to 14 hours a day working in our shop.

When the gals get tired looking at the four walls in the trailers, they come out and look at us. Marieanne and Lynn are very different but they get along pretty well. Oh sure, there's some conflict. But as long as we can all live this close and not have any more than an occasional small tiff, we're in good shape.

We have a pretty neat setup now. You should have seen this place when Don first picked it out. It was a mess. About 70 to 80 percent of the land was overrun by poison ivy.

Don is recognized as one of the top mechanics around. One year he came in second in the voting to pick the best big car mechanic of the year. He and I were voted midget driver and mechanic of the year in 1967 and I got the Eddie Sachs Award in 1973 for being the driver who best exemplifies racing and set the best example.

Don and I are fortunate to have the folks we have. They really set the blueprint for us. My dad's thin and wiry. He's a good person who has been willing to help in any of the causes that Don or I might have. He's very dedicated, and was the type of guy who would never cheat on his boss regardless of the situation. Before he retired, dad was the kind of guy who would work 20 hours a day if he had to and never complain. In fact, he just about killed himself working so hard, lifting too many heavy things by himself. Dad feels people should be treated the way you'd like to be treated yourself. He has passed that trait on to us.

My mom not only is a good cook but she really helped me with my school work, especially helping me to memorize stuff. I had a very poor memory when I was younger and still do. If I don't write something down, I won't remember it the next day. You'd probably have to consider my mom as the more dominant personality of my parents. The blend of her liberalism and my dad's conservatism worked out very well for Don and I when we were growing up. We probably got things a little earlier, thanks to my mother's urging, than we would have gotten them, if it had been left up to my dad alone.

My folks are real fine people. I just wish I could get them to go to church on a steady basis and speak out for the Lord. I haven't been able to do this, no matter how hard I've tried. It's been an impossible task. The same thing is true with Don. You know it's a funny thing. I can talk to strangers about the Lord and get them to proclaim their belief in Jesus Christ. But I can't do the same thing with my loved ones. My folks believe in Christ but I don't think they've ever confessed that belief verbally. I think it helps to express your belief in Christ whenever you can. Maybe my folks express their belief to each other. I don't know, and maybe it's none of my business. I like to think that they're going to the right place. And maybe they are.

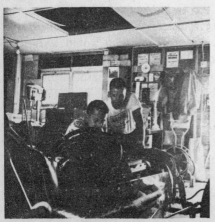

Mel and Don working

Dad looking things over

Rebuilding the engine

Chapter Eleven

We Get Caught Cheating

There's one chapter in my racing career I'm not too proud of. It took place at Joliet, Ill., in 1962 while I was competing in a United Auto Racing Association event. Don and I tried to slip one over on UARA. I drove a midget that had an illegal Ford tractor engine. Here's how the whole business came about.

The tractor engines were legal in Florida. I drove the midget that had the tractor engine in Florida in the winter of 1962. I really mopped up. I entered 23 races and won 18 firsts, two seconds and one third. About the only bad thing that happened to me down there was when I spun out in one race. I won the NASCAR midget division championship that year in Florida and won it decisively. I was raking in as much as $224 a night. I won enough money in four nights of racing to pay for our whole two-week vacation at Daytona Beach.

When we came back to the midwest, I ran a couple of races with the legal engine we had. One race, however, I lost a piston. I wanted to race this one particular weekend in a series of races in the Chicago area. But my problem was I didn't have a car to drive which had the proper engine. Don and I talked it over and we decided we'd use the illegal Ford tractor engine. We knew what we were doing was wrong, but we figured we could get away with it. Some figuring!

We did, too, the first night, anyway, at Santa Fe Park Speedway near Chicago. I finished third in the feature. I'm sure I could have done better but I didn't want to arouse anybody's suspicions. I just played it cool and easy. Joliet was the next stop Saturday night. I had the fast qualifying time although I didn't go all out. I had to drop out of the trophy dash and heat race because my car wasn't handling properly. Don and I worked on it and got it running okay in time for the feature. Early in the race, I passed quite a few "hot dogs" on one corner. By hot dogs, I mean local racers. This kind of upset them. My illegal tractor engine had nothing to do with me passing them. It was just that they were making some silly mistakes. The guy who was leading was almost a straightaway ahead of the pack. By then, I'd moved up to second place. Don came out to the track and gave me a little hand signal to "cool it." So I did, resigning myself to finishing second.

I really wouldn't have minded if the other drivers would have passed me, I didn't want to attract any more attention than I'd already drawn. But nobody passed me. Wouldn't you know it, the guy leading the race made a bad goof. He swung very wide, permitting me to catch up with him. It looked like he was deliberating making mistakes so he'd lose. He swung very wide a second time, allowing me to shoot into the lead.

I knew then that I'd been set up but I said to myself, "Oh, heck, as long as they're going to let me win, I'll see how fast I can go." Well, that illegal Ford tractor engine went pretty fast, let me tell you. I went so fast that I set a new track record, won the race, got a nice trophy and a kiss from this pretty queen.

That's when all heck broke loose. The guy who had been leading the race promptly protested my victory and he was joined in by several other irate drivers. Some of these guys had raced down in Florida and had seen me drive the tractor-powered engine down there. I'm convinced they let me win, so they could later protest. None of the officials inspected my car at the track that night. Don and I were staying at the house of an official who would have to check over the motor. I guess he figured he could check the motor at his house the next day. Don and I didn't sleep very well that night. We knew the officials had us dead to rights. I saw no way we could beat the rap. The next morning, Don and I yaked back and forth with this official. Finally, he said it was time to quit talking and time for him to inspect our engine.

"That won't be necessary," I told him. "The engine's illegal." I figured we'd at least get some appearance money for competing at Joliet. But the "powers that be" there said we wouldn't get a penny since our car wasn't kosher. That made Don and I very mad. But there wasn't anything we could do about it. After all, we were the guys caught with our hands in the cookie jar. We were suspended for six months from racing at Joliet.

Right after that little fiasco, we took our tractor

engine to Sun Prairie. I won the feature race there, too. And this time I got paid because the tractor engines were legal at Sun Prairie. After that race, we decided to sell our tractor engine to the highest bidder. We got a pretty good price for it. That engine had developed quite a reputation. It brought me 10 firsts in 14 starts. Not to mention one big hassle.

Selling that engine meant we were in the market for a new one. I wasn't about to stay in UARA, not with that six month suspension staring me in the face. I joined the United States Auto Club, and have been a member of USAC ever since. Before I joined, however, I looked up Howard Linne. He was one of the biggest car owners in USAC at the time and still is. We asked him if we could rent an Offy engine from him for $2,500 and 25 percent of all we made. Now, car owners don't normally rent out engines, they sell them. An Offy engine cost about $5,000 and we simply didn't have that much money. Linne agreed to our offer. He'd seen me race previously and had been impressed. Otherwise, I'm sure he wouldn't have rented us his Offy engine. I did quite well in the remaining USAC races that year, finishing fifth in the national point standings.

That fall, Don and I scraped up enough money to buy the engine from Linne for $2,500 and we took it to California for the racing season there. In my very first race in California, I blew the engine. Howard Linne again came to our rescue, selling us enough parts to put our engine back together for the 1963 season.

In the fall of 1963 I'd gone out to race in Arizona and California by myself. Don stayed home to get married. I'd become friendly with Johnny Pouelsen, who was the chief mechanic for Parnelli Jones. So when I was out in

California, I stayed with Johnny Pouelsen at Compton. I slept in my own camper, which was parked at the airport where Pouelsen's 500 Flying Club was headquartered. I worked on my midget and also helped Parnelli get his car ready. Then I went out and beat Parnelli Jones in the Midget Grand Prix at Gardenia, Ca.! Parnelli didn't like that one bit. In fact, he was so mad after the race that he rammed his car into the pit fence. Nope, he didn't congratulate me. As I recall, he didn't say a thing to me. I certainly wasn't about to say anything. I made it a point not to sleep at Johnny Pouelsen's that night. I stayed in a motel.

As for the race itself, I started out the Grand Prix in eighth position. Gradually, I worked my way up to second behind Parnelli. Just as I was about to make my move and pass him, his magneto went sour. I passed him as if he was standing still. I lapped Parnelli to win the race going away. I picked up a nice piece of change. J. C. Agajanian gave me a big trophy, I got a kiss from the trophy queen and nothing but stares from Parnelli. I'll never forget that win.

1st win after Langhorne

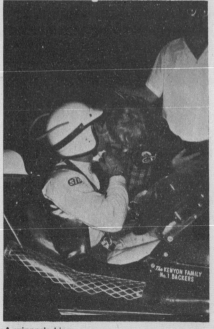

A winner's kiss

Chapter Twelve

I Get Married Again

In 1963, a very important person came into my life. My wife Marieanne. Marieanne's from Geneseo, Il. Her maiden name was Neumann. I met her while I was roller skating at a rink in Moline, Il. She was working at the time as a commercial artist in Moline. You might say we met by accident. We were skating in a dance called the "Bell Skate." A boy and girl pair off and skate together until they blow a whistle. Then, the guy moves forward to skate with another gal. Well, Marieanne was my partner several times that night on the "Bell Skate." There was something about her that I liked right away. I think the feeling was mutual on her part. We didn't start dating immediately, though, because I had to go to Florida to race and then later to Canada.

When I got back from Canada, I looked her up and we had our first date. You wouldn't call our first date very exciting. I took her home to show her my race car and meet my folks. Marieanne had never seen a race car before and she was impressed. I even got her to climb into my car. Later on, I took Marieanne to several races with me. The first race I took her to was at Freeport. When I picked her up, I was wearing my race togs. "You sure look funny in that blue monkey suit," she told me. I told Marieanne that all drivers wore these blue monkey suits. After she'd seen how the other drivers looked in their suits, she decided I looked quite handsome in mine. Marieanne got a pretty good idea of my life-style as a race driver. I wanted her to know all about racing. I failed to do this in my first marriage and it proved to be a mistake.

Marieanne and I clicked, even though she was 10 years younger. We had a lot of the same likes and dislikes. We both liked to go to church, roller skating, movies and neither one of us minded staying home and spending a quiet night. She liked doing things outdoors, and so did I. There was nothing shy about me while I was courting Marieanne. Racing had done a lot to help me get rid of my shyness. I knew I wanted Marieanne to be my wife and I was bound and determined that she would be. Three months after our first date, I gave her an engagement ring. Nine months later we were married. We were married on April 12, 1964 in St. John's Lutheran church, in Geneseo.

One might say April has been a lucky month for Marieanne and I. Her birthday is April 9, mine is April 15 and we were married on April 12. We really had a big wedding. There were over 300 people who came to the wedding. My brother Don was my best man, and Hal Schroeder was a member of the wedding party. He was the only race driver who attended the wedding.

Marieanne made her own wedding dress, and she and her mother made the dresses for her attendants. I'll never forget our wedding day. The weather was miserable. It was cloudy, windy and rained all afternoon.

Marieanne and I were the lucky ones. We got away from all that bad weather the next day and headed for Daytona Beach. We spent our honeymoon there, soaking up the sunshine and romping on the sandy beaches. We went to an amusement park once and had a ball riding those electric bumper cars. I guess Marieanne wanted to show me she was a pretty good driver in her own right, too. She showed me all right. She belted me around pretty good. I got in some of my own licks, too. But I must admit she won that round. We've had a beautiful marriage. We've had a few differences of opinion. What couple doesn't? But we've never had an out-and-out-fight where we've refused to talk to each other for days and days.

Marieanne brought me much closer to Jesus Christ. I'll always be grateful that the Lord put somebody in my life like Marieanne.

Marieanne and my wedding

Qualifying Indy 71 sprite.

Chapter Thirteen

From Midgets to Big Cars

I've been asked more than once why I decided to start driving championship cars. It's nothing I planned on doing. It just happened. In 1963, Johnny Tawl of Crown Point, In., asked me if I wanted to drive a big car in the Trenton 150 that fall. Johnny was the chief mechanic for the car. I didn't have anything to lose, so I said, "Sure, why not?" I went to Trenton with great expectations. After doing so well in the midgets, I didn't think I'd have any trouble driving big cars. It didn't take me long to realize, however, that there's quite a difference between driving midgets and driving big cars. In those days, the big cars were big dinosaur roadsters, not like the narrower rear engine cars that you have today in the championship cars. Everything about that roadster was different than the midgets I'd been used to driving. For one thing, I was sitting beside the drive shaft, instead of straddling it. The steering was also different.

The big cars were much heavier and had much more horsepower. It was almost like having driven a pick-up truck all one's life and then suddenly started driving a semi.

I didn't do too well in qualifying, but I did make the starting field for the Trenton 150. When the green flag was dropped, I stomped down hard on the throttle. That roadster jumped right out from under me. It started to zigzag down the straightaway and I almost lost control. I said to myself, "Well, do something, Dummy!" I grasped the steering wheel as tight as I could and gave it a hard shake just as if I was driving a midget. I don't know why but it worked. My big roadster straightened out and I went on to finish twelfth. I didn't consider that a bad way to start my big car career. I was also scheduled to race in the Trenton 200 that same fall, but a conflict came up and I had to skip that race.

I didn't drive a big car again until the 150 miler at Milwaukee the week after the Indy 500 in 1964. I drove Dick Kemerly's roadster, the same car in which I was badly burned in at Langhorne the following year. This roadster was a much better car than the one I'd driven at Trenton earlier. It had the same suspension as our midget, and it was much easier to steer and handle. I finished fifth. That was the same race in which Jim Hurtubise was badly burned. He was running third when it happened. I was back in tenth place at the time. Little did I realize that I'd be badly burned and following Hurtubise to the same Burn Center in San Antonio a year later almost to the day.

All told, I ran in six big car races in 1964 but finished only three of them. Seems like one little thing after another kept happening to prevent me from doing well. For instance, at Trenton I was running a strong third when a fifteen cent bolt in my throttle broke. In the 200 miler at Milwaukee, by brakes burnt out and then as I went into the No. 3 turn, I spun out. At Phoenix, I was running second behind Don Branson. I felt I could pass him anytime I wanted to because I had a faster car. But I dropped a valve and was forced out on the 140th lap while Don went on to win the race. I did get a lot of valuable experience driving big cars that year. And I also got the opportunity to get to know and get some valuable tips from guys like Branson, Chuck Rodee, A. J. Foyt and Parnelli Jones. I worked on Parnelli Jones' pit crew at Indianapolis in 1963 and 1964 and then after I was bumped from the qualifying field at Indy in 1965, I also helped Parnelli's pit crew.

In 1965, I was under contract to drive a front engine big car for Federal Engineering at Detroit. Those front engine old dinosaurs were just on their way out then. The independent suspension, rear engine racers were the coming thing.

As I mentioned earlier, I got bumped on the last day of the Indy qualifying that year. I had high hopes, however of doing well in the next race at Milwaukee. I had told the people at Federal Engineering that if their car didn't run any better at Milwaukee than it did at Indianapolis, I'd have to get me another car. When we got to Milwaukee, my car was completely changed. I couldn't even drive it. By the time we got the chassis changed around to where I could at least go around the track, it still wasn't running right. As a result, I failed to qualify for the 150 miler at Milwaukee. I was plenty mad and disgusted. I broke my contract with Federal Engineering and decided to drive the same roadster I drove for Dick Kemerly in 1964.

The next stop in the big car circuit was Langhorne. Before I went there, however, I won a couple seconds competing in midget races in Ontario, Canada and Fort Wayne. I was leading a midget race at Jackson, Mich., but blew an engine. After racing at Fort Wayne, I drove all night to Langhorne with Les Scott and a friend of his. Two days later, I was in a hospital with third degree burns all over my body. Not too long after that, Jesus Christ became the focal point in my life.

The skid at Langhorn Pa.

The crash coming

Chapter Fourteen

A $20,000 Pit Stop

1967 was a very good year for us. I placed sixteenth in the Indy 500 and won the national midget championship, winning 17 USAC feature races. It was the second time, I'd been the top midget driver. All this just whetted my appetite. I wanted to do even better in 1968. The year didn't start out well for our 3-K team. Fred Gerhardt, who owned our Indy type car, told us that unless we came up with a sponsor, we couldn't race his car. He told us this on April 1. This left us in a real jam. It's tough enough as it is getting a sponsor six months before the Indy 500, but here it was only two months before the big race and we didn't have a sponsor. All of our prospects were pretty well dried up. Out of desperation, I went to the City Council in Lebanon and asked them if they couldn't do anything for me. Lebanon's quite a sports town. It's the hometown of

Rick Mount, the former Purdue All-American basketball player. On such short notice, the City Council told me they couldn't do anything official. But they did agree to advertise our plight in the newspapers and on the radio. They staged a big campaign, asking people to contribute anything they could. People from all walks of life, boy scouts, truck drivers, businessmen, paper boys, contributed money to our cause. They raised $4,000 for us. That was a fantastic sum for a town of only 10,000 to come up with on a strictly voluntary basis in a short, three-week period. What was even more amazing was the fact, we'd only lived in Lebanon for a year and really didn't know that many people. Well, we had our sponsor and called our car, "The City of Lebanon Special." Now the rest was up to us.

We had all sorts of problems before and during the qualifying for Indianapolis. We burned two pistons and overhauled the engine not once, but twice. In addition, our front end kept pushing out, especially on the corners. It was hot and windy on the first day of qualifying. On my first qualifying attempt, I was waved off the track by Don because I simply couldn't get up enough speed. I tried several more times to get up speed but couldn't do it. I never did take the green flag to make an official qualifying attempt. We decided to wait until Sunday and try to qualify then. On Sunday, the rains came and so we were forced to wait until the second weekend of qualifying.

It rained quite a bit during that week while we were waiting for the second weekend of qualifying. I practiced when it wasn't raining. And once when it was raining, we decided to overhaul the engine a third time. Come Saturday, it looked like I had good enough speeds to qualify. But my front end was pushing out badly on the corners. Despite this, Don gave me the "Go" sign for my second qualifying attempt. Nothing came of it. Don waved me off again with the yellow flag. That meant that we had only one last chance left to try to qualify.

Sunday was the last day of qualifying. There were several spots still open. I was still having trouble cornering. Some people from Goodyear came up with an idea. They suggested that we change our wheel sizes from a 16-inch to a 15-inch in an effort to keep the front end from pushing out. You have to run the same size tires in the race as those you qualify with. I called the Goodyear people out in California to see if those size tires would be available to us on race day. They said Yes. Then I went and borrowed 15-inch tires from Gordon Johncock to use during qualifying. Before I changed tires, I was straining to reach 162 miles per hour. With the new tires, I was running laps at around 166 miles per hour. When I went out on the qualifying line for my third and last attempt, I felt that Harlen Fangler, the chief steward, and I were like old friends since I'd been on the line so many times.

Since the fire, I have also prayed and asked the Lord to give me strength and guidance. I'll admit I was pretty frustrated at this point, but I sought Christ's help and understanding. I knew that God's will, not mine, would be done, whether we qualified or not. I did qualify, however, with a speed of 165.191 miles per hour. That was high speed for that day and was worth $1,000 in itself. It put me in the seventeenth starting position.

After supper that night, Don and I went back to the Speedway to check over our engine. We discovered that one of the cylinders had a 70 percent leak. It had a three-inch crack, which accounted for the fact our car was hard to start. We couldn't believe it because the block was only a week old. Each block is worth $5,000. We had to get a new block. We didn't know where we were going to get one. We certainly didn't have $5,000 laying around to buy one. And none of the other people in the garage area had a spare block.

And they weren't about to loan us a $19,000 engine, especially since I might use it to beat their entry, or worse yet, wreck it. At the last minute, Goodyear came to our rescue again. They loaned us a test engine which they had used in Roger McCluskey's car.

I started the race light, meaning I had only 30 gallons of fuel aboard instead of the full load of 70 to 75 gallons. We were required to make the mandatory three pit stops but we were hoping I could come in during a yellow flag to refuel and not lose too much time. That yellow flag never came. Finally, Don gave me the sign to come in for fuel. As I was coming off the fourth turn, I ran out of gas and had to coast in to the pit area. I didn't think this was any big thing, but soon found out otherwise. While the guys in my pit area were refueling, they discovered that our starting cables were about three inches short. They couldn't get the cables to reach my car. Everyone scurried around frantically before we got things straightened out and my car started again. I was in the pits for a precious one minute and 55 seconds. Usually, pit stops take only 25 seconds or less.

Anyway, I finished third, some 55 seconds behind Dan Gurney, who was second. That one minute, 55 second pit stop cost me second place. If we hadn't goofed around so long in the pits, I would have beaten Gurney. That long pit stop cost us $20,000—the difference between second and third place. We did get $49,000, which was my best finish ever at Indy.

I finished fourth at Indianapolis in 1969 and fourth again in 1973. But the Indy 500 I'll never forget was 1971. That was the year the pace car rammed into the press stand, scattering photographers and writers all over the place. I didn't hear about that crash until later. I had a lot of other things on my mind, namely the hairiest thing that's ever happened to me.

It took place very early in the race, on the eleventh lap I think. Steve Krisiloff had just blown his engine and spilt oil and water all over the track. He didn't hit the wall, but just left all that oil as his calling card. I was about to enter the third turn when I noticed the smoke on the short chute. I went into that turn as I normally would. That was a big mistake on my part. I didn't see all that oil on the track until it was too late. I spun and careened along the wall for about 100 feet before I hit the wall with my rear end, flattening the left rear tire. My car wasn't really damaged too much, only about $300 worth. The yellow light was on and I was taking my time getting out of the car.

There was one fireman on each side of me and another one was coming toward me down the track. I unhooked my harness, slid my feet back and was two-thirds of the way up in the cockpit, ready to climb out of the car. I looked up and here comes Gordie Johncock bearing down on me like a runaway freight train. I said, "Oh, no," and quickly dropped down into the cockpit. I closed my eyes tight. I was sure I was a goner. I could feel myself being shaken around violently. Then everything stopped suddenly. I opened my eyes and I was still there. I was amazed, flabbergasted. I couldn't believe it.

I didn't know where Gordie or the three firemen went. My car around me was completely destroyed. It was a mess. There was 60 gallons of fuel running down the track away from me. I quickly popped my fire bottle. I think that's what kept my car from catching fire. Fortunately, it was nose down. My car's dash was wrapped around my shins. But there were no broken bones. I was fortunate in that respect. When I got out of my battered car, I noticed that my right boot was halfway off. I didn't know how that happened. I hobbled down into the infield and my right leg started hurting something awful. Anytime a driver hits a wall, it's mandatory that he goes to a hospital to get checked. As I went by the main grandstand, I tried to wave to Marieanne but she didn't see me. When I got to the hospital, it was completely full. "You'll have to take a seat and wait your turn," somebody told me. That's exactly what I did. I didn't know the photographer's stand had been demolished by the pace car. As I was sitting there, I took my boots off and saw some blood and a hole on my shin bone. It was just a small one and it took only three or four stitches to close it. I was very lucky. I could have been killed after Gordie rammed me broadside. When I took my helmet off after I got into the infield, I saw this big tire track right across my helmet. It was Gordie's tire track all right! I was that close to getting finished off. Gordie came over to the hospital while I was getting sewed up and apologized all over the place. I told him to forget it. He certainly didn't mean to do it. The sad part of it was that Gordie and Johnny Rutherford and been battling each other back and forth. They'd raced through two or three yellow flags before they ran into the slick oil spot on the corner that I'd hit. They were severely reprimanded for trying to pass under the yellow flags. Oh yes, one final thing about that crash. Remember those three firemen that Gordie almost ran over? Well, they promptly quit on the spot. I can't say that I blamed them.

Gordon Johncock #7 tire going over my head

Not much left of 71 Sprite car

Don and Mel waiting to qualify

Chapter Fifteen

What it Takes to be a Driver

On numerous occasions, I've been asked what it takes to be a good race driver. First of all, it takes good reflexes, nerves and a competitive spirit. The real pros can get in a bad predicament on the track and get out of it if their car is still rolling on four wheels. And our pulse rates don't change. It's definitely safer to drive on a track than on a freeway even though going at speeds of up to 200 miles per hour on a straightaway.

I've spun and hit the wall during a race and hardly worked up a sweat. But I've had close calls on the freeway, and my heart has dropped clear into my mouth and went clang, clang, clang! As a rule, race drivers know what they're doing. You can't say the same thing for everybody on the highway. We go as fast as we feel comfortable. If trouble should arise, we compensate for it, or hit the wall. It's as simple as that. All drivers wear the best equipment possible. And the cars are built in such a way that unless it catches fire, chances are you won't be killed.

USAC drivers come in all shapes and sizes and they cover almost every personality imaginable: the hot heads—the guys who get mad on a regular basis, and those drivers who never get mad or flustered.

I try to get close to other drivers, but most drivers don't. They don't want to become too involved for fear another driver might be killed. I can truthfully say I'm friends with most drivers. I can sit down and talk with almost all of them. None of the drivers call me preacher, or anything like that. At least not to my face. Christians often have problems with people who don't share their beliefs. But that's not true in my business. In racing, everybody has a tendency to let everybody else alone. Racing does give me a tremendous opportunity to witness over the public address system during qualifying for the Indianapolis 500. Every time I've qualified at Indy, I've always made it a point to thank my Lord for being with me and guiding me around that place. Qualifying is always the toughest thing about Indy.

There have been times when I've driven my four qualifying laps at Indy and can only remember driving the first lap. Somebody was helping me drive that thing, and it had to be God.

Drivers, especially the well-known ones, have all sorts of good-looking women chasing after them. If a driver wants to go that route—and most do—they have plenty of opportunities to play around. There are gals who would gladly give up their virginity just to be associated with a big time race driver. How do I resist temptation? I keep busy. There's lots of drinking and partying that goes on among the racing crowd. I rarely go to these parties because they always end up to be drunken brawls. It's not only the drivers who get drunk but people in general. I don't like to be around drunks. Most drunks make asses of themselves. And besides, I really don't have any time for partying. I'm a working driver. By that, I mean I actually work on the engine and chassis, help load the car and work on it. When you are a working driver, you don't have much free time to fool around. After I'm done racing, I'm usually so tired that all I'm interested in is getting a hot shower, a meal and some sleep.

About the only other driver I can think of who is a working driver is A. J. Foyt.

I don't talk to the other drivers about Christ unless they bring it up themselves. If I tried to force my Christianity upon these guys, they'd rebel. Most of them don't feel the way about Christ I do. Most drivers are interested in nothing but driving as fast as they can and partying. I can relate very easily to drivers who've been hurt badly. Jim Hurtubise and I were teammates in 1966 but we never had an opportunity to get in a serious discussion.

Mel and A.J. Foyt

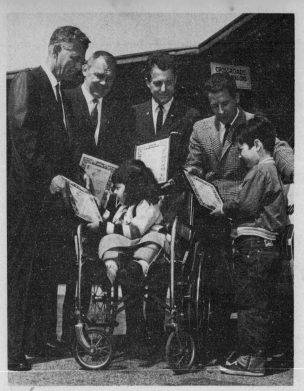

Fred Agabashian, Gene Heartly, Mel, and Mario Andretti
at Crossroads Rehabilitation Center

Johnnie Rutherford, Roger Ward, Mayor Lugar,
Bobbie Unser, Art Pollard, Mel and Al Unser

Chapter Sixteen

A. J. Foyt and Other

Drivers

A. J. Foyt is one of the best all around drivers I've competed against. He drives everything. Parnelli Jones was good in his time, but among the active drivers, A. J. is the best. Al Unser is probably the second best driver.

Many members of the press don't like A. J. They think he's rude, a hot head and very uncooperative. What many of them don't do is try to understand A. J. He's a working driver, and doesn't have much free time for the fans and sportswriters. It is surprising at the demands fans place on a driver. I try to talk to everybody and keep moving on. Some fans, though, are never satisfied. They keep badgering you and won't let up. They feel since they bought a ticket they own a piece of you. And if they can't get a piece of you, they get very mad. I know that from experience. There have been times when I've finished answering a question from one fan, and turned to talk to somebody else. Then, I've had the first fan butt in and try to ask another question while I'm still talking to this other person. This can get very aggravating.

You can't blame A. J. when he blows up and tells somebody in no uncertain terms to get lost. And I can readily understand why there's a sign on A. J.'s garage at Indianapolis which says, "Keep Out. No Admittance."

Why is A. J. the best driver? Because he's so versatile. He knows an engine inside out, and knows how to squeeze out as much speed from it as possible without picking it up and carrying it around. When I say picking it up and carrying an engine around, I mean someone who can make his car look better than it actually is through his driving skills. A driver who can do that, expecially in qualifying, is Bobby Unser. Mario Andretti is another who can do that. Mario won his first big car championship, and then learned to drive. I had predicted that if Mario didn't get killed before he won a championship, he could become a good driver. And he has become a good driver.

Being a big car champion does something to a driver. It changes a person because he finds his time isn't his own anymore and he's constantly in demand. This is what first got A. J. into trouble with the press. I know how many demands are placed on me and I've never won the Indy 500. I can just imagine how much more the press and fans pester those who have won at Indianapolis. I'm sure their time is chopped up into little chinks, and they have very little time to themselves. If they are not being interviewed by somebody, they are making an appearance somewhere, or scheduled to drive at another place. All this constant pressure and being on the go changes a person. It makes you a little more hostile and wary toward people, in general, and newspaper people, in particular.

Sometime ago, Bobby Unser published a book in which he evaluated every driver. Well, I don't plan to do that in this book. I know Bobby didn't have too many nice things to say about my style of driving. He said if he had to drive like I do, he simply couldn't do it. Sure, I'll admit I'm a steady driver. I drive to finish. Bobby drives to be first.

Getting back to Mario Andretti, Mario and I started racing big cars about the same time. I'd say until I got burned at Langhorne, we were about on par. In fact, until the fire I think I was doing better than he was. Unfortunately:or fortunately depending on how you look at it—I was burned and he went on to greater things. Mario became a champion, but I think in the end I became a better person because of being burned. It brought me to the realization that Jesus Christ is my Lord and Savior. As a committed Christian, I've experienced the real blessings and saving grace which God has freely given us through his Son.

Who looks where they're going?

Upside down, San Jose

Chapter Seventeen

Midgets Are For Me

Harvey Duck, a sportswriter for the *Chicago Daily News*, interviewed me last August and asked which I liked better: Driving midgets or Indy type big cars. I had to be honest and said midgets. It's the only type of motorsports racing left that is fun. I'm not saying this just because I've won a record 77 midget feature races, and am the only four-time USAC midget driving champion. Indy car races are all business. There is no fun. Only work. Road racing is getting to be the same thing. Only the midgets give me a kick anymore, like I got this past year when I finished third in the midget standings.

Driving a midget is a flat out, foot-to-the-floor type of thing. It's close competition. It's not a long endurance race like big cars. You've got to go flat out or you don't make it. With big cars, you pick a speed and hope to finish. But in midgets you step on the gas and hope to win. It's definitely a lot more fun driving a midget. On the average, you run a midget three or four times a week. You work on midgets just as long as you do the big cars. But you run them more often for the same amount of work. You usually run only once a month in a big car. I'll admit that you can run all year in a midget and not make as much money as you could possibly make in one big car race.

But money isn't everything, although I have made as much as $28,000 in one year driving a midget. When one works for an Indy car owner, you work approximately 90 hours a week for 40 hours pay. You are working day and night for somebody else. Don and I talked it over and we just felt that we were working too many hours for somebody else. That's when we decided to go into the midget business for ourselves. Not only do we race midgets, but Don, my father and I build them too in our garage in Lebanon. Midgets on the average cost about $14,000. The most we've sold in one year is five. When we first started selling midgets, we made between 12 and 20 percent profit. Now that we're making most of the pieces ourselves, we can make as high as 60 percent profit.

Driving midgets requires more skill than driving an Indy type car. The driver makes much more difference. In midgets, your reflexes have to be quicker and sharper. Sure, you're running faster in Indy cars, but your reactions are a great deal slower. Midget tracks are a great deal shorter. Sometimes they are used four nights a week. After a few years, the dirt on the track becomes so saturated with oil and rubber, it loses its freshness. So you've got to work that much harder. It's really tough physically.

Tires are a much more critical factor in midgets than at Indianapolis. Then too, the tracks differ so much that you are always changing suspension setups. Sometimes, you don't have much time to practice, so you end up guessing and hoping that you've hit on the correct setup. Still there's that feeling of accomplishment that you get after running well in midgets that can't be duplicated anywhere else. I've had 22 years of it and I know very well that I'll miss it when I quit. Big cars are more demanding than midgets. After 10 years of driving big cars, it became kind of a drag because of the hours spent on the silly things for the amount of times it was run.

Driving midgets may be more enjoyable now than ever because of the new pickups and motor homes. They allow one to bring the family along with a bit of comfort and without spending a lot of money. I have a 20-foot motor home that will sleep six, and four very comfortably. I take Marieanne and our two sons, Brice, 3, and Vaughn, 5, with me when I'm out on the midget circuit. It costs us on the average of $1.22 per day per person to eat when we are on the road in our motor home. When the boys grow older, I'm sure it will cost more. The reason our food costs are so low is that Marieanne does a lot of planning. We bring most of the food with us from home when we travel. We eat a lot of hamburger, because it is fast to prepare. Of course, we sleep in the motor home, so that cuts costs a lot, too.

Chapter Eighteen

Racing in New Zealand,
Australia

Not too many people can combine a vacation with work. I'm lucky, I've been able to. For five of the last seven years, my family and I have spent our winter vacations in beautiful New Zealand and Australia. We were there in 1970, '73, '74, '75, and went again this last December. This last time Marieanne and the kids and I were there six weeks. We flew there early in December and spent five weeks in New Zealand, and the other week in Australia. This year we stayed in a six-room villa in Auckland, New Zealand. That villa was something else. It was situated right on the ocean. The beach was only about a quarter of a mile from our villa. We all spent a lot of time soaking up the sun, swimming and romping up and down the beach. New Zealand and Australia are great places to relax and go for a vacation.

At the same time, I've been able to run a lot of midget races in those countries. Only they don't call it midget racing there but Speedcar racing. I've done real well, too. A year ago, I won the world midget driving championship and won 15 out of 20 feature races. Don't ask me how many feature races I've won in Australia and New Zealand down through the years, because I can't honestly tell you. I know I've won a lot of races.

The fans in New Zealand and Australia are tremendous. The fans come to see a person perform. In this country, fans are different. When they buy a ticket, the fans sometimes feel like they've bought a piece of you. They seem to think you owe them a certain period of time for chatter, or whatnot. In New Zealand and Australia, the fans respect the drivers more.

The New Zealand and Australian drivers are handicapped because of the equipment they use. In New Zealand, the equipment is about three to five years behind our equipment. In Australia, it's about two years behind ours. One thing about those New Zealand and Australia drivers, they certainly have tremendous desire. But sometimes they let their desire get the best of them and they do foolish things and get in our way or crack into us on the tracks.

A year ago, four American drivers drove in the midget circuit in Australia and New Zealand—myself, A. J. Foyt, Larry Rice and Gary Patterson. All four of us were back there again this winter.

The grandstands and pit areas in Australia and New Zealand are every bit as good as the ones we have in the United States. I can't say the same thing about their tracks, however. The dirt tracks there are generally poor One reason for this is because they use them for both motorcycle and midget races. You really can't mix the two types of racing. The surfaces are so bad that they will wear out a set of tires in one or two nights. In the United States one can get by for six or eight races on one set of tires.

Speedcar racing in Australia and New Zealand is superior to American midget racing in one important aspect: the crowds there are much, much bigger. It's normal for them to have between 25,000 and 27,000 people turn out to watch a championship Speedcar race. In the States we are fortunate if we get a crowd of five or six thousand for a championship race. They probably average about 12,000 fans a night for their races.

New Zealand champions

Leading A.J. FOYT and GORDON JOHNCOCK

Chapter Nineteen

Burned to Life

It was during these three months in San Antonio that Jesus Christ became real to me. He is always near to me now in every moment of my life. My faith was strengthened when I felt the presence of the Lord during my struggle to live. I thought about these things while I reflected upon Hal Schroeder's unfortunate suicide.

When I was hospitalized, I realized that life has more to it than just fame or fortune, that life should be lived by following Jesus Christ's example. I felt Jesus' healing hand upon me when I was doing well, and I also felt his strength and courage when my pain and frustrations were overwhelming.

Marieanne's faith was severely tested during this trying experience, but it was strengthened because of it. We both realize that our purpose in life is to witness our renewed faith in a God who is made known to the world by the saving grace of our Lord and Saviour, Jesus Christ.

Looking back, one might say what happened to me when I was burned was a blessing in disguise. Even though, I lost my fingers, I found Jesus Christ. And that had made a big and wonderful difference in my life.

People have asked me how I became a Christian. I went to Sunday school every week, and was brought up in the church. My mother was Catholic, and my father was Congregational. I was brought up as a Presbyterian, and eventually became a Lutheran.

Before the fire, I had never really accepted Jesus Christ as my Saviour, or become an active Christian. I looked on going to church as a duty. It had no real meaning.

A change came over me while I was recuperating at the San Antonio Burn Center. It wasn't an instant conversion, or immediate thing, or anything like that.

I was getting along well at the hospital. Most of my grafting had been done and I was healing exceptionally fast. This came as a surprise to the doctors there. When they first took me to the Burn Center, a dozen doctors predicted I'd be hospitalized for nine months. Most of the time, doctors there are very accurate with their predictions.

But, here it was, just two months after I entered the hospital and I was well on the road to recovery. Then, I developed a very bad infection and it spread all over my body. I think God was trying to tell me something. I wasn't getting the message, however.

When I first entered the hospital, bandages were not used to cover my burns. I was covered with sheets, like a mummy.

I was in an open ward. There's a special reason for this. Most burn patients can't push bells or buzzers with their burned hands to summon somebody. If you need anything, all you do is holler out, "corpsman or nurse."

When the infection appeared, the only part of my body that was still covered was my left hand. I'd been burned so badly that I needed skin grafts all over my body. My donor sites, where they'd taken off some skin and put it elsewhere, started pumping fluid like crazy. The doctors couldn't figure out why this was happening. This was probably the first time I'd really run into pain and itching. My bed was full of scabs every morning. I itched constantly. Tranquilizers were given to keep me calm. But they didn't help.

I was a mess. Puss bags and pockets formed all over my body, sometimes up to three inches long. When this happened, they'd have to cut the bags open with a scissors and scrape out all the puss and junk. My body was oozing out so much fluid every morning that it ran over the edge of my bed and onto the floor. I didn't envy the people who had to clean up around my bed.

To make matters worse, the donor sites on my back became angered so much that they almost became burns themselves. I couldn't lie down to sleep. I had to sleep sitting up on a rubber thing shaped like a donut, while holding my badly burned left hand high in the air. Trying to sleep in this awkward position was difficult. It was almost more than I could bear.

To be perfectly frank, I spent a lot of time crying and feeling sorry for myself. I made life miserable for everybody around me, especially Marieanne. Every time a chaplain would come into my ward, I'd call to him. I didn't care what faith he was. I just wanted to see if maybe he could crank up something for me.

At this time, I never really did think Christ had deserted me. But I must admit I was disillusioned. I put time out of my mind. I didn't know what day it was, or what meal was coming next. Time became completely obliterated in my mind.

Marieanne would come to the hospital every day to feed me. She'd feed me in the morning, again at noon, and again at night. She did this for over a month. The fact Marieanne is a Christian helped get it through my thick, stubborn head that I needed help. I couldn't do it by myself. We prayed a lot together.

Marieanne never actually told me so in so many words, but it dawned on me that I wasn't getting any better. I was getting worse. I was terrified that I'd lose my skin grafts and have to start the whole sickening process all over again. That was the biggest blow to me. Finally, I made up my mind that I needed Christ's help to lick this thing. With Marieanne's help, I fully accepted Christ into my heart and turned my life over to him. I can't recall exactly when or how I made this decision. There was no big clap of thunder, or bands playing, or anything like that to signal my conversion.

Several days later, however, there was definite improvement in my condition, both spiritually and physically. It was as if the dark clouds had been swept away and the sun had come into my life. I still had my itching problem, but at least my infection had cleared up.

Something deep inside me told me I had turned the corner. My body was healing remarkably fast. Shortly thereafter they uncovered my left hand. Earlier, they had worked on the ends of my fingers. Now they wanted to work on my fingers some more.

Before they could do this, however, I had to sign another paper and give them permission to cut off more of my fingers. The circulation wasn't good yet in my fingers. They told me they would use their own judgment as to what my circulation problems were before deciding if they had to do any more cutting. Every time they cut off more of my fingers, I said to myself, "Well, this is going to make it more difficult for me to ever consider racing again."

I didn't lose confidence in God or abandon hope of racing again. I thought about a good driver friend of mine, Alan Heath, and received inspiration from his story. Alan has a hook for an arm, but he still drives. Now as a child of God I knew I'd be driving USAC again.

Checking the wheels

Chapter Twenty

From Racing to Witnessing

How long will I keep racing? I'll keep on driving as long as it's fun. When it becomes a job and a chore, I'll quit racing and probably become a mechanic. I'd like to keep driving for a long time. I'm not old. I just turned 43 in April. I know of a driver, Ted Hartley, who raced until he was 67. I'm looking forward to driving at Indianapolis this year. I'm hoping to work out a deal with A. J. Foyt so I can either buy a car from him, or drive one of his cars. I've never said I've wanted to do anything before, but I definitely want to win the Indy 500. I think it would be a fantastic thing for a Christian to win that race. It would have an impact on other Christians who might be wavering in their faith, or leaning the other way.

Racing has been very good to me. It's been the major part of my life. Sure, I've lost the fingers on my left hand, and a lot of skin, but in their place I've gained friends all over the world. And I've also gained the greatest friend of all, Jesus Christ. I've probably gotten more out of racing than I've put into it. I have a beautiful family, great parents, a wonderful wife and a tremendous brother.

I'm not the greatest public speaker in the world, but if I wanted to I could probably work full time going around the country making speeches for the Fellowship of Christian Athletes, Youth for Christ, Campus Life and various church groups. Unfortunately, because of my heavy work load and racing commitments, I have to curtail my speaking engagements.

I've spoken to diverse groups all over the country. I spoke before an Indiana Highway Patrol Convention once, and also spoke before a Cigarette Industry Convention. Every time I speak, I always talk about my personal relationship with Jesus Christ. I'm not a professional speaker and don't preach or give sermons. I just try to witness my faith as best I can and tell about my experiences as a driver. I make it a point to say that my faith in Christ was inactive and dormant before I was badly burned at Langhorne. But through this shattering experience, I explain that I came to know my Lord as my Saviour. I became a committed Christian who knows the real blessing and saving grace which God made available to us through His Son, Jesus Christ. The Lord means a lot to me, and I rely on his guidance and strength in everything I do, especially when I'm driving at the famed Indianapolis Motor Speedway. I never hesitate to tell people all of this.

I can't quote Scripture very well and don't try to conceal this fact from groups I'm speaking to. I do read the Bible and try to relate what I read to my daily life. I try to live my life according to the Ten Commandments and to the new commandment which Jesus introduced when he told the people, "to love the Lord thy God with all thy heart, and with all thy soul, and with all thy mind, and to love thy neighbor as thyself."

The more I become involved in my Christian faith, the more I realize my shortcomings and inadequacies. I pray to the Lord, asking his forgiveness and ask him to use me as a witness despite all my faults. Marieanne and I have come to know and love God through His Son and our Saviour, Jesus Christ. I do hope and pray this story of my life will in some way be an inspiration to others, and that others can get to know Christ, without having to go through an unfortunate experience like I did.

Tragedy often strikes because of our mistakes and human frailties. But God is with us even during those trying times. I know that is true because I experienced it firsthand after being burned. I get my kicks or highs out of racing, rather than out of a bottle, or pill, like some other people. It's a tremendous thrill for me to race at speeds of over 200 miles per hour and then zoom through a corner. When that happens, I say to myself, "Wow, I made it! Let's try it again." But all of my racing goals are really secondary to my primary goal. And that's to be the best Christian witness possible for my Lord, Jesus Christ.

Postscript

Not only is Mel Kenyon a dedicated race driver but he's also a dedicated Christian. This book has presented his life story. However, not too much was said about Mel's actions, which best exemplify and characterize his Christian faith. He was much too humble to recount or mention many of his good deeds. We'd like to mention just one, which really shows the type of warm, concerned human being he is. It was told to us by Chester Miller of Bloomington, Il. Miller, of course, is the person who wrote the poem, "Practice and Qualification". Miller had the poem printed on pocket cards which Mel passes out at races as a form of witnessing, and we'd like to share it with you.

Practice and Qualifications

Throttle, Torque, and Traction, friend
　　Will set you on the pole.
They're an added blessing
　　Everywhere you go.
It would help an awful lot
　　If you would just make one pit stop.
And ask the Lord to share
　　Everything He's got
Patience can be yours you know
　　Courtesy to others show.
You can even smile.
　　When friends go by.
Pleasure's tach goes out of sight
　　When everything is set up right.
Because you know He is The Way
　　The Truth – the Life.

Getting back to the story that Chester Miller told us. It concerns a nine-year-old boy, Dale Vasselin and his older brother, Larry, 16, of Morton, Il. The two were riding on Larry's motorcycle one day. They were looking for Dale's bicycle, which had been stolen. They were two blocks from their house when a car ran a yield sign and hit them broadside. There was a fire and explosion. Larry was killed almost instantly. Dale was critically burned over 85 percent of his body, and rushed to a hospital.

When Miller read about this tragic accident in the

Bloomington newspaper, he realized that there was only one man he knew who could encourage young Dale Vasselin in the critical time, and that was Mel Kenyon.

Miller had become acquainted with Mel at the Indy qualifications in 1966. Miller called Mel at Lebanon and told him what had happened. In the meantime, some friends came over to Miller's house from Morton. They immediately spotted the only copy of the *Christian Athlete* magazine that Miller had. It featured a story on Mel Kenyon, called, "A Witness At The Wheel." They took that magazine to the hospital where Dale was very critical. They were feeding him intravenously. Dale's mother read him Mel's story once. He said, "Mom, read it again." She read it a second time. Dale kept asking that the story be read to him again and again. Finally, his mother transcribed Mel's story on a cassette tape recorder. That way, Dale could listen to it anytime he wanted to. Dale made this statement, "If Mel Kenyon can do it, I'll try."

A short while after that, two letters arrived at Miller's home almost simultaneously. One was from Mel Kenyon, addressed to Dale Vasselin. The other letter was from young Dale. It was addressed to Mel Kenyon, but sent in care of Miller. It was unsealed. In it, Dale asked for three things, some word from Mel, his picture and his autograph. Mel's letter was sealed but Miller later learned that Mel's letter to Dale contained exactly those three things he wanted! What would you call that, coincidence? Miller called Mel's letter a sanctified message. Mel also sent flowers to Dale.

Dale began to improve and things were going well for him. He was actually released from the hospital for a short while. But then to the surprise of everyone, he became critical again, and he died in November, 1970, some five months after his accident. Before hs died, Dale made a tape for Miller and the junior department in Miller's church. On the tape, Dale said he wanted three things: he wanted to see Mel in person, he wanted to visit Miller's junior department at his church, and he wanted to live to be 10 years old. He did live to see his tenth birthday but that was all. His birthday was on November 20. He died the next day. All the time he was in the hospital, he kept telling the anxious doctors and nurses, "It's all right if I die, I'll go right to heaven."

Marieanne and Mel showed their feeling and heartfelt concern for Dale's family by sending them a beautiful bouquet of flowers and a note.

The thing that really surprised Miller took place at Indianapolis the following May during qualification trials for the Indy 500. Miller and a friend were walking down "Gasoline Alley." As Miller passed Kenyon's garage, he spotted Mel and five other members of his crew working frantically on one of his three cars. Miller turned and started to walk away, figuring Mel was too busy to talk.

Miller heard someone holler, "Chet, come in here." It was Mel. He walked in and the first words that Mel told Chet were: "Marieanne and I are sorry that we lost Dale Vasselin." Miller and Mel chatted briefly before Miller left Mel's garage. When he and his friend, Tom Taylor, got outside the garage, they looked at each other and were struck by the same thought.

"How many other people under the same circumstances would have even remembered our names and said what Mel did about Dale Vasselin?" Miller asked Taylor. "That is the real measure of Mel Kenyon as a man. He was responsible for three cars, hadn't qualified yet, and it was the last week of qualifying. Yet, he took time out to talk to us."

This story is just one of many that illustrates what type of person Mel Kenyon is. He's not afraid to share his Christian faith. And as A. J. Foyt said in his introduction, "Mel is as nice a person as you would want to meet on or off the track."

500 Flags - Both Sides **

Green is "Go"
Go forward in life with all you've got. Praise Him and steer your life around Him.

Black is "Come in for Consultation"
Come to Him for guidance and consultation through prayer.

Yellow is "Caution"
Be very careful in moving ahead in difficult times. Just maintain present speed until things clear up.

Blue Stripe is "Move Over, Someone is Passing"
Notice it says move over. A step sideways is easier to make up than one back, and safer. Life has many sidesteps but we learn from them and become better people and winners.

124

White is "One More Lap"

That last important move toward the end. Having lived a full life, in prayer, and completed things here on earth, we take the last step toward future life.

Checkered is "Winning"

We are all sinners in the eyes of the Lord. For when we follow the other colors and have Him on our "pit crew" you can't help but come out ahead.

**This poem written by Mrs. Elizabeth Byrkett of Indianapolis, In. and sent to me in the spirit of prayer, is a guideline I use to relating my Christian faith in my daily life.*

Mel meeting President Nixon

RECORDS

Mel Kenyon has established many USAC midget lap and individual records in the 14 years he's been with USAC. The following are USAC records Mel still holds as of January 1, 1976. We are indebted to Donald Davidson and USAC for providing these records.

Mel Kenyon is: the only four-time USAC Midget Champion

the USAC Midget Division All-Time Point Leader

the USAC Midget Division Feature Winner Leader—77 feature wins

the USAC Midget Division Single Season Most Midget Feature Wins—17 wins in 1967.

Mel Kenyon places 23 in the USAC Championship Division All-Time Point Standing.

USAC Midget Division Track Records Established by Mel Kenyon

(Laps)   (Date)   (Time)   (Speed)

Trenton International Speedway (1 1/2 Mile Paved), Trenton, NJ

1 Lap*   6/17/72   39.95   135.169

Indianapolis Raceway Park (5/8 Mile Paved), Clermont, In.

10 Laps   8/20/75   4:00.96   93.377

Tri-City Speedway (1/2 Mile Dirt), Granite City, Il.

40 Laps   7/20/69   17:53.77   66.435
Speedway "605" (1/2 Mile Paved), Irwindale, Ca.
100 Laps 11/30/75 40:50.20   73.463
Illiana Motor Speedway (1/2 Mile Paved), Schererville, In.
8 Laps   8/3/75   2:51.42   84.004

*Records Established in Qualifications

Capitol City Speedway (1/2 Mile Paved), Madison, Wi.
1 Lap*   8/27/69   19.07   94.389
6 Laps   8/27/69   1:55.30   92.072
8 Laps   7/17/70   2:36.80   91.837
30 Laps 7/27/69   9:45.19   92.278
Manzanita Park Speedway (1/2 Mile Dirt), Phoenix, Az.
50 Laps   4/8/67   19:44.00   76.013
100 Laps 11/20/71 41:54.96   71.572
Salem Speedway (1/2 Mile Paved), Salem, In.
40 Laps   5/29/72 12:49.00   93.628
81 Speedway (1/2 Mile Dirt), Wichita, Ks.
40 Laps   6/20/74 13:48.03

Colorado National Speedway (3/8 Mile Dirt), Erie, Co.
12 Laps   8/8/73   4:28.24
Merritville Speedway (3/8 Mile Dirt), St. Catherines, Ontario, Canada
1 Lap*   7/6/75   16.978
Weedsport Speedway (3/8 Mile Dirt), Weedsport, NY
1 Lap*   7/3/75   18.285
4 Laps   7/3/75   1:14.74
Columbus Motor Speedway (1/3 Mile Paved), Columbus, Oh.
50 Laps   6/2/74   13:09.32

Hales Corners Speedway (1/3 Mile Dirt), Hales Corners, Wi.

  1 Lap*   8/15/75   17.664
  4 Laps   8/15/75   1:13.36

Fairgrounds Motor Speedway (1/3 Mile Paved), Louisville, Ky.

  3 Laps   7/25/71   45.80

Ascot Park (1/4 Mile Dirt), Gardena, Ca.

  10 Laps   4/17/65   2:57.52

Kokomo Speedway (1/4 Mile Dirt), Kokomo, In.

100 Laps   5/30/65 30:10.54

Manzanita Park (1/4 Mile Dirt), Phoenix, Az.

  8 Laps 11/22/70 1:54.27

Rockford Motor Speedway (1/4 Mile Paved), Rockford, Il.

  4 Laps   6/1/72   56.97
  10 Laps 6/28/68 2:22.80
  50 Laps 7/20/67 12:04.18

Indianapolis Speedrome (1/5 Mile Paved), Indianapolis, In.

  1 Lap*   8/8/75   12.791

Memorial Coliseum (1/10 Mile Paved), Fort Wayne, In.

  1 Lap*   1/25/70   8.27

In 14 years in USAC midgets, this is how Mel Kenyon has finished. (in point standing)

1962 - 5	1969 - 2
1963 - 2	1970 - 12
1964 - 1	1971 - 20
1965 - 8	1972 - 10
1966 - 2	1973 - 7
1967 - 1	1974 - 1
1968 - 1	1975 - 3